The Official PrintMaster Guide

Michael Miller

A Division of Macmillan USA
201 West 103rd Street, Indianapolis, Indiana 46290

Trademarks

Warning and Disclaimer

Publisher
John Pierce

Development Editor
Susan Hobbs

Managing Editor
Thomas Hayes

Project Editor
Natalie Harris

Copy Editor
Julie McNamee

Indexer
Sharon Shock

Proofreaders
Maribeth Echard
Bob LaRoche

Technical Editor
William Fike

Team Coordinator
Lori Morgan

Interior Design
Kevin Spear

Cover Design
Maureen McCarty

Layout Technician
Mark Walchle

Production Control
Dan Harris
Heather Moseman

Contents at a Glance

Contents

10 Better Projects with PrintMaster's Special Tools 119

Part 3 Get Creative: How to Create Different Types of Projects   129

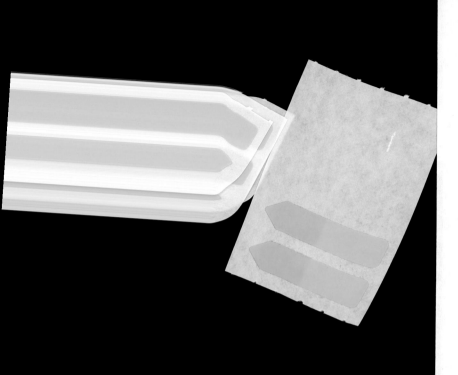

10 Better Projects with PrintMaster's Special Tools 119

About the Author

Michael Miller is a writer, speaker, consultant, and the President/Founder of The Molehill Group, a strategic consulting and authoring firm based in Carmel, IN. More information about the author and The Molehill Group can be found at www.molehillgroup.com, and you can email the author directly at author@molehillgroup.com.

Mr. Miller has been an important force in the book publishing business since 1987. In his most recent position of Vice President of Business Strategy for Macmillan Publishing, he helped guide the strategic direction for the world's largest reference publisher and influence the shape of today's computer book publishing market. There are few who know as much about the computer industry—how it works, and why—as does Mr. Miller.

As the author of 30 best-selling nonfiction books, Mr. Miller writes about a variety of topics. His most recent books include *The Complete Idiot's Guide to Online Auctions, The Complete Idiot's Guide to Online Search Secrets, Sams Teach Yourself MORE Windows 98 in 24 Hours*, and *Webster's New World Vocabulary of Success*.

From his first book (*Ventura Publisher Techniques and Applications*, published in 1989) to this, his latest title, Michael Miller has established a reputation for practical advice, technical accuracy, and an unerring empathy for the needs of his readers. Many regard Mr. Miller as the consummate reporter on new technology for an everyday audience.

Tell Us What You Think!

As the reader of this book, *you* are our most important critic and commentator. We value your opinion and want to know what we're doing right, what we could do better, what areas you'd like to see us publish in, and any other words of wisdom you're willing to pass our way.

As a Publisher for Que, I welcome your comments. You can fax, email, or write me directly to let me know what you did or didn't like about this book—as well as what we can do to make our books stronger.

Please note that I cannot help you with technical problems related to the topic of this book, and that due to the high volume of mail I receive, I might not be able to reply to every message.

When you write, please be sure to include this book's title and author as well as your name and phone or fax number. I will carefully review your comments and share them with the author and editors who worked on the book.

Fax: 317-581-4666

Email: office_que@mcp.com

Mail: Publisher
          Que
          201 West 103rd Street
          Indianapolis, IN 46290 USA

Introduction

What do you want to make today?

Do you need new business cards? How about some personal letterhead? Want to send a greeting card to someone? Or while away the time with a crafts project? Maybe you're really ambitious, and want to create your own personal Web page?

Whatever you want to make, PrintMaster will help you make it. PrintMaster is America's best-selling home graphics program, and an endless source of projects for your home or small business. My only complaint with PrintMaster is that there's just *too much* you can do with it!

How do you figure out everything PrintMaster has to offer—and how to use all of its powerful tools? To get the most from PrintMaster, you need a guide—something to help you do all you want to do without getting lost or messing something up.

This book is your official guide.

What You'll Find in This Book

The Official PrintMaster Guide is written for anyone currently using any version of PrintMaster, including new PrintMaster 8.0. With this book, you'll learn everything from PrintMaster basics to advanced design techniques—while getting the inside scoop on how to best use the program to create your specific projects.

To help you get the most from PrintMaster, this book is organized into four major parts, as follows:

> **Part 1—Get Started: How to Start and Use PrintMaster.** In these chapters, you learn all about the PrintMaster Design Workspace and how to create, save, and print your projects.

> **Part 2—Get Productive: How to Build Better Projects.** In these chapters, you learn how to add and edit different types of elements in your projects, including backgrounds, text, lines, drawings, pictures, and photographs.

> **Part 3—Get Creative: How to Create Different Types of Projects.** In these chapters, you learn about all the different projects you can make with PrintMaster, including projects for kids, for the home, and for small and home-based businesses.

> **Part 4—Get Online: How to Use PrintMaster with the Internet.** In these chapters, you learn how to access the resources on PrintMaster's Web site, how to send online greeting cards, and how to create and publish your own personal Web pages.

In addition to the step-by-step information presented throughout the book, *The Official PrintMaster Guide* also includes additional tips and hints to help you enhance your projects. This additional information is presented in three different forms:

PrintMaster Tip

These tips present inside information on ways to use PrintMaster to more effectively and efficiently accomplish the task at hand.

Internet Tip

These tips contain Internet-related information—including the addresses of Web sites that contain resources you can use in your PrintMaster projects.

Design Tip

These tips contain stylistic advice to help you make your projects look better and be more effective.

Written with the blessing and assistance of the program's creators, *The Official PrintMaster Guide* is an indispensable tool for any PrintMaster user!

Let Me Know What You Think

I always love to hear from my readers—that's where I get some of the best ideas for my books! If you want to contact me, feel free to email me at **books@molehillgroup.com**. I can't promise that I'll answer every email, but I will promise that I'll read each one!

If you want to learn more about me and any new books I have cooking, check out my Molehill Group Web site at **www.molehillgroup.com**. Who knows, you might find some other books there that you want to read!

PART 1

Get Started: How to Start and Use PrintMaster

Chapter 1

Welcome to PrintMaster

PrintMaster—published by Broderbund, a division of The Learning Company—is the number-one, best-selling home graphics program today (1998 PC Data retail unit and dollar sales). Every day, millions of people use PrintMaster to create cards, calendars, posters, and crafts for their homes and small businesses.

PrintMaster is easy to use, and creates great-looking items and projects—especially if you have a decent color printer as part of your computer system. You can use PrintMaster's built-in graphics and photos, or import your own pictures and photographs to spice up your projects; you can even go online and download tens of thousands of additional images from PrintMaster's Online Art Gallery!

You don't have to be a computer expert or a professional designer to work with PrintMaster—in fact, most projects can be completed by clicking a few onscreen buttons and choosing premade design templates. Just choose your project, select a design, and enter your specific information—you're ready to print!

Even though PrintMaster is extremely easy to use, I've written this book to help you get even more value from the program—to create better-looking projects more easily. Read on to learn more about the PrintMaster program—and how to make it work for you!

What PrintMaster Is—And What It Can Do for You

PrintMaster is a graphics program that lets you create a wide variety of projects and pieces. If you participate in any community activities or events; if you run a small or home-based business; if you want your own personalized holiday and greeting cards; or if you like working with crafts, you'll love how PrintMaster helps you create the materials you want and need, quickly and easily. And if you have kids—well, between the fun craft projects and the useful Homework Helpers, you'll wonder how you ever got by without your family's copy of PrintMaster!

Just look at the types of projects you can create with PrintMaster:

➤ Banners

➤ Brochures

➤ Business cards

➤ Calendars

➤ Greeting cards

➤ Certificates

➤ Crafts

➤ Envelopes

➤ Fax cover sheets

➤ Forms

➤ Fun for Kids

➤ Garlands

➤ Homework Helpers

➤ Invitations

➤ Kitchen crafts

➤ Labels

➤ Letterheads

➤ Matching sets

➤ Newsletters

➤ Online greeting cards

➤ Notecards

➤ Photo projects

➤ Postcards

➤ Posters

➤ Web pages

Although PrintMaster essentially provides you with a "blank slate" on which you can place all types of pictures and text, it also automates the process so that most projects can be created with a few clicks of your mouse. PrintMaster is so easy to use, anyone—even your kids!—can create great-looking projects the first time they use the program.

You start with one of PrintMaster's thousands of ready-made projects (as shown in Figure 1.1), and then edit the elements within the project to your liking. You can add and delete graphics, resize and recolor elements, enter your own text, insert your own photographs, and even create stunning visual special effects. The result (as shown in Figure 1.2) is a project that looks like it was designed by a professional; no one will know you did it yourself, on your own personal computer and color printer!

To put it another way—PrintMaster lets you make a lot of stuff—fast!

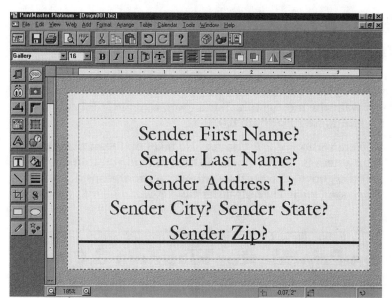

FIG. 1.1

Start with a ready-made project...

Platinum, Gold, and Classic—The Different Versions of PrintMaster

Several versions of PrintMaster are available today. Generally, the higher-priced the version, the more graphics included and the newer the version number, the more tools included. So, if you want the most graphics and tools, buy the latest edition of the higher-end version—PrintMaster Platinum 8.0.

Of course, the most complete version of PrintMaster also takes up the most disk space on your computer. If your system is short on hard disk space (and you think you might not use all the graphics provided with the Platinum version), consider buying one of the lower-priced versions, such as PrintMaster Gold 8.0.

Focusing on PrintMaster Platinum 8.0

In writing this book, we couldn't write in detail about all available versions of PrintMaster—we had to pick a specific version for the book's step-by-step instructions. Because PrintMaster Platinum 8.0 includes all the features available in all the other versions, we picked this version to focus on in this book. If you have one of the other versions of PrintMaster, realize that some of the features discussed here might not be available with your software.

Table 1.1 shows the features of all the currently available versions of PrintMaster.

Note that all the versions within a specific version number (8.0 or 7.0) feature the same basic program and operations, so you won't sacrifice basic functionality by purchasing a lower-priced version. You just won't get as many graphics or the same add-on tools, both of which can help you create more interesting projects.

You can purchase any of these PrintMaster programs wherever software is sold, or directly from The Learning Company's ShopTLC Superstore (on the Web at new.shoptlc.com, or by phone at 1-800-973-5111).

Table 1.1 PrintMaster Version Comparison

	PrintMaster Platinum 8.0	PrintMaster Gold 8.0	PrintMaster Platinum 7.0	PrintMaster Deluxe 7.0	PrintMaster Publishing Suite 7.0	PrintMaster Classic 7.0
PrintMaster Graphics: Total Images	160,000+	100,000+	150,000+	75,000+	12,000+	8,000+
Photographs	27,000+	25,000+	10,000+	1,000+	150	
Original Master Art	4,000+	3,000+	3,200+	2,200+	2,000+	600+
National Geographic Premium Photos	100	100	100	100	0	0
Premade Project Templates	8,500+	7,000+	8,000+	6,400+	4,300+	1,300+
Sentiments	2,500	2,200+	2,000	2,000	2,000	0
Fonts	600	600	250	250	250	250
DrawPlus	Yes	Yes	Yes	Yes	Yes	Yes
Photo Organizer	Yes	Yes	No	No	No	No
Photo Workshop	Yes	Yes	No	No	No	No
Headlines	Yes	Yes	No	No	No	No
Homework Helpers	Yes	Yes	No	No	No	No
Kitchen Crafts	Yes	Yes	No	No	No	No
Seals and Timepieces	Yes	Yes	No	No	No	No
Animated 3D Greetings	Yes	Yes	No	No	No	No
Automatic Event Mailings	Yes	No	No	No	No	No
Web Page Creation	Yes	Yes	Yes	Yes	Yes	Yes
Minimum Disk Space Required	310MB	175MB	170MB	125MB	70MB	60MB
Suggested Retail Price	$59.95	$39.95	$39.95	$29.95	$19.95	$9.95

What's New in PrintMaster 8.0

If you're a PrintMaster 7.0 user, should you upgrade to PrintMaster 8.0? You might want to think about it; the new version includes a lot of new features, as well as more graphics, projects, and fonts. Just look at the new features of PrintMaster 8.0:

➤ **Animated Greetings.** Personalized online greeting cards you can send to your friends via email.

➤ **Enhanced Art & More Store.** Easier operation and larger selection in PrintMaster's Online Art Gallery.

➤ **Headlines.** New special effects for your headlines, including colors, textures, shadows, and more.

➤ **More artwork.** More artwork of every type, including photographs, original Master Art, and special artwork for Web sites.

➤ **More and better fonts.** Hundreds of new fonts, including Drop Caps.

➤ **More projects.** Hundreds of new and different projects, including Kitchen Crafts and Homework Helpers.

➤ **More sentiments.** Hundreds of new greetings and messages for your cards.

➤ **New photo-editing tools.** Two new tools—Photo Organizer and Photo Workshop—to help you organize and edit photos for use in PrintMaster projects.

➤ **New Web features.** Dozens of new ready-made Web pages, as well as a tool to preview animated GIF files on your Web pages. In addition, PrintMaster can now convert *any* project into HTML so that it can be uploaded to the Web.

➤ **Seals and Timepieces.** Official-looking seals and fun clocks you can add to any PrintMaster project.

The main reason I recommend upgrading to PrintMaster 8.0 is the addition of the new photo-editing tools. With home scanners and digital cameras getting lower-priced and easier to use, it's easier than ever before to add your own photographs to your PrintMaster projects. With Photo Organizer and Photo Workshop, you can not only organize and manage all your photographs, but also crop and clean up your photos to look their best when you print them out.

PrintMaster's Tools and Galleries

In addition to the main PrintMaster program, different versions of PrintMaster offer a variety of additional tools and galleries that let you do even *more* with your projects. Some of the tools and galleries you have access to are listed here.

➤ **Address Book.** PrintMaster's Address Book holds the names and addresses of your friends and family—and you can merge your Address Book contacts into personalized holiday cards, invitations, labels, and more.

➤ **Art & More Store.** The Art & More Store enables you to obtain additional art-work from PrintMaster's Online Art Gallery. You can preview and purchase tens of thousands of new drawings and pictures online, and then download your purchases for immediate use within the PrintMaster program. The following collections are available online: Bedtime Stories, Fanciful Holidays, Janet Carder, Nostalgic Valentines, Victoriana Christmas, and New Year's Eve.

➤ **BorderPlus.** The BorderPlus tool lets you create unique borders for your projects, using any artwork from PrintMaster's Art Gallery.

➤ **Cartoon-O-Matic.** This tool creates unique comic faces you can insert into your projects; you pick the face you want, and then modify any and all facial elements to your liking.

➤ **DrawPlus.** DrawPlus is an easy-to-use drawing tool that lets you modify PrintMaster's built-in artwork or create your own drawings.

➤ **Event Reminder.** This is a useful tool that monitors your Address Book and notifies you of important upcoming dates—birthdays, anniversaries, and so on.

➤ **Headlines.** This new tool lets you add Ready-Made or Custom headlines to your projects, using a wide variety of stunning professional effects.

➤ **Photo Organizer.** New to PrintMaster 8.0, this handy tool lets you organize your photos so that you can quickly locate the ones you want for your PrintMaster projects; Photo Organizer also lets you create electronic albums, produce slideshows, and attach photos to your email.

➤ **Photo Workshop.** Also new to PrintMaster 8.0, Photo Workshop lets you edit and repair the photos you add to PrintMaster projects.

➤ **Project Gallery.** This gallery consists of ready-made designs you can use to start new projects.

➤ **Seals.** This tool lets you add official-looking seals to certificates, awards, and other PrintMaster projects.

➤ **Sentiment Gallery.** This gallery consists of hundreds of sayings, phrases, and messages to add spice to your projects.

➤ **Timepieces.** This tool lets you create unique "clocks" you can use to announce a specific time in your invitations, announcements, and other PrintMaster projects.

➤ **Web Art Gallery.** This gallery contains special artwork—including buttons, backgrounds, horizontal rules, and animations—you can use when creating your personal Web pages.

➤ **Year You Were Born.** This fun tool provides historical information for any specific date—terrific trivia for birthday cards and calendars!

You use these tools and galleries within PrintMaster to add pizzazz to your projects. And they're all as easy to use as the main PrintMaster program itself!

In the Next Chapter...

Now that you've learned what PrintMaster is, turn to Chapter 2, "Find Your Way Around," to discover how PrintMaster works!

Find Your Way Around

PrintMaster is so easy to use that most versions don't even come with large printed instruction manuals. Still, if you're like most users, you want to have some type of help available when you first start using a new program. If you're a new PrintMaster user, then, this chapter is for you. Just read on to learn how PrintMaster works—and how to start creating your first projects, step-by-step!

Print a User's Guide

PrintMaster comes with an electronic User's Guide, which you can print out as needed. Just pull down PrintMaster's Help menu and select Show Help Window. When the Help With PrintMaster window appears, select the Contents tab, select Before You Start, and then select PrintMaster User's Guide. When the User's Guide appears, select a specific topic from the pull-down list, and then click the Go button. When the topic appears, click the Print button in the Help toolbar.

Starting and Exiting PrintMaster

When you install PrintMaster, it should install a PrintMaster menu on the Windows Start menu, as well as a PrintMaster icon on the Windows desktop. You can start PrintMaster by selecting the icon on the desktop, or by clicking the Start button, and then selecting PrintMaster.

The first time you start PrintMaster, you are asked to enter some personal information—your name, address, birth date, and so on. Go ahead and enter this information, because it helps automate the data entry for some PrintMaster projects. (And feel free to leave any fields blank—you'll still be able to use PrintMaster even with empty data fields!)

Edit Your Personal Information

You can edit your personal information at any time by pulling down PrintMaster's Tools menu and selecting Sender Information. When the Select Sender dialog box appears, select your name and click the Edit button. (You can also add a new "sender" by clicking the New button, or delete a "sender" by clicking the Delete button.) When the Sender Information dialog box appears, move from field to field (either with the Tab key or by repositioning your cursor), changing or adding data as you like; click OK when done.

 Depending on how you installed PrintMaster, you may be asked to insert the Program CD to proceed. (Minimal installations don't install all the program files to your hard disk, and thus, need to access the CD for some operations.) In addition, as you access specific art galleries from within PrintMaster, you are prompted to insert specific Art CDs. Because most of PrintMaster's graphics are stored on CDs (and *not* automatically installed to your hard disk), you'll want to have all your PrintMaster CDs handy when you use the program. If you don't have the right CD, PrintMaster won't be able to proceed as directed.

To exit PrintMaster, first save any open projects you're working on by clicking the Save button on the File toolbar, or by pulling down the File menu and selecting Save. Then, pull down the File menu and select Exit. (If you have any unsaved projects open, PrintMaster prompts you to save them before it lets you close the program.)

Recognizing the PrintMaster Desktop

Now, let's take a quick tour of the PrintMaster desktop, and all the elements you see there. If you ever get lost and don't recognize a desktop element, you can refer to this section of the book, or let your cursor hover over the item in question. Hovering over an item displays a ToolTip that tells you what the element is.

Hints and Tips

As you use PrintMaster, you'll see a variety of hints and tips popping up in little onscreen windows. To close a hint or tip window, click the Close (×) button in the window's top-right corner. If you want to turn off these hints and tips completely, pull down the Help menu and *uncheck* the Show Helpful Hints and Show Design Tips options.

The Design Workspace

The basic PrintMaster window, shown in Figure 2.1, is called the *Design Workspace*. Any project you're working on appears in its own *project window* within the Design Workspace, and you use the toolbars attached to the Workspace to add or edit individual elements within your projects.

Elements of Success

Any individual part of a project—graphic, text box, line, border, picture—is called an *element*. As explained in Chapter 5, "Better Designs," any element can be edited in various ways—resized, recolored, rotated, and so on.

If you start a project from scratch, the project window in the Design Workspace appears blank—until you add elements to your project, that is. If you start a Ready-Made project or open an existing project, all the elements of the project appear in the Workspace.

Work on Multiple Projects at the Same Time

PrintMaster lets you work on multiple projects at the same time; each project appears in its own individual project window within the overall Design Workspace. To arrange multiple project windows, pull down the Windows menu and choose from Cascade (which stacks windows one on top of another), Tile (which arranges windows horizontally), or Arrange Icons (which arranges the icons for any minimized projects at the bottom of the Workspace).

FIG. 2.1

PrintMaster's Design Workspace—where you work on all your projects.

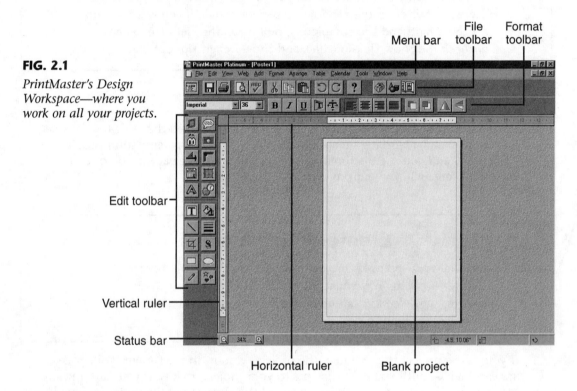

The Menu Bar

Most of the functions in PrintMaster can be accessed from the pull-down menus on the menu bar. To select a menu function, just pull down the appropriate menu and then select an option; if the menu item has an arrow to the right, there is a *submenu* of additional options available.

Table 2.1 details all the functions available from PrintMaster's menu bar.

Table 2.1   Menu Functions

Menu	Available Functions
File	New, Open, Close, Save, Save As, Revert to Saved, Export As, Print Preview, Print, Print Setup, Double Sided Print Setup, Print Alignment, Acquire, Select Source, Send, Send Online Greeting, Cancel a Scheduled Online Greeting, Preferences, Online Preferences, Free Offer, Exit. (Note: Up to four recently opened files may also be displayed on this menu.)
Edit	Undo, Redo, Cut, Copy, Paste, Paste Special, Duplicate, Select All, Delete, Delete Pages, Edit Banner Text, Find\Replace Text, Import Text, Replace Object, Photo Workshop, Edit Border, Edit Drawing Object, Merge Names, Replace Picture, Choose Postcard Type, Choose Label Type, Choose Envelope Type, Links, Object.
View	Percent View, Fit in Window, Fit to Window Width, Fit to Window Height, Zoom In, Zoom Out, Zoom to Area, Zoom to Selected Toolbars, Rulers, Guides, Text Box Outlines, Front, Inside, Back, Go to Page, Go to Master Page, Hide Master Page.
Web	Page Properties, Web Publishing Properties, Hyperlink, Create Hot Spot, HTML Text Format, Design Checker, Publish to Folder, Publish to Web Site, Preview Web Site, View Web Site, Go to PrintMaster Site.
Add	Picture, Border, Drawing Object, Sentiment, Cartoon-O-Matic Picture, Object, Custom Graphics, Picture from Disk, Web Art, Text Box, Free Draw, Line, Rectangle, Ellipse, Shape, Table, Headline, Mail Merge Field, Pages, Add Page Number.
Format	Fill Color, Line, Shadow, Text Shape, Crop, Reset Crop, Font, Character Spacing, Paragraph, Tabs, Bullets & Numbering, Drop Caps, Insert Symbol, Insert Date, Text Box, Bold, Italic, Underline, Stretching, Horizontal Alignment, Vertical Alignment.
Arrange	Position, Layer, Select Previous Object, Select Next Object, Mirror Left to Right, Flip Top to Bottom, Text Wrap, Group, Ungroup, Snap to Rulers, Add Guide, Snap to Guides, Lock Guides.
Table	Autoformat, Cell Formatting, Insert, Delete, Fill Down, Fill Right, Merge Cells, Split Cells.
Calendar	Month and Year, Calendar Style, Edit Calendar Title, Date Number Font, Weekday Name Font, Edit Date Text, Choose Date Picture, Date Picture Color, Clear Date.
Tools	Check Spelling, Address Book, Import Address Book, Select Merge Names, Event Reminder, Sender Information, The Year You Were Born, Print Pictures from Disk, Fill-In Fields.
Window	Cascade, Tile, Arrange Icons. (Note: All open projects are also listed on this menu.)
Help	Show Help Window, Preferences, Show Helpful Hints, Show Design Tips, Recent Hints, About.

As with all Windows applications, not all functions are always available. If a menu item is grayed out, the function isn't available during your current operation.

You can activate many PrintMaster commands directly from your keyboard; they do not require using a mouse to select menus and options. After you learn these keyboard shortcuts, they can save you time. The following table lists the keyboard shortcuts available in PrintMaster.

Function	Shortcut Keys
Add a new Address Book entry	Ins
Copy	Ctrl+C *or* Ctrl+Ins
Cut	Ctrl+X *or* Shift+Del
Delete	Del
Format bold	Ctrl+B
Format italic	Ctrl+I
Format underline	Ctrl+U
Help	F1
Move cursor left one word	Ctrl+Left arrow
Move cursor right one word	Ctrl+Right arrow
Move cursor to beginning of line	Home
Move cursor to beginning of text	Ctrl+Home
Move cursor to end of line	End
Move cursor to end of text	Ctrl+End
Move element down	Down arrow
Move element left	Left arrow
Move element right	Right arrow
Move element up	Up arrow
New	Ctrl+N
Next window	F6
Open	Ctrl+O
Paste	Ctrl+V *or* Shift+Ins
Previous window	Shift+F6
Print	Ctrl+P
Redo	Ctrl+Y
Save	Ctrl+S
Select All	Ctrl+A
Undo	Ctrl+Z *or* Alt+Backspace
Zoom in	+
Zoom out	-

Workspace Toolbars

Although you can always access PrintMaster's functions via the menu system, you can also access the most important functions from one of PrintMaster's three toolbars. These toolbars—File, Format, and Edit—each contain buttons that perform a specific function when clicked. Most users find it quicker to click a toolbar button than to pull down a menu to perform the same function.

How to Hide or Display Toolbars

To hide or display any toolbar, pull down the View menu, select Toolbars, and then put a check mark by the toolbar(s) you want to display; uncheck any toolbar you don't want to display.

The *File* toolbar is the first (top) toolbar at the top of the Design Workspace. The buttons on this toolbar are used to display the Hub (which is kind of like a master control panel for starting PrintMaster projects), save and print projects, edit text and other elements, display PrintMaster's Help, and access various PrintMaster tools. These are the most-used functions in PrintMaster, and you'll access the buttons on this toolbar often. Table 2.2 details the buttons on the File toolbar, and what they do.

Table 2.2　File Toolbar Commands

Button	Name	Function
	Hub	Displays the Hub.
	Save	Saves the current project to disk.
	Print	Prints the current project.
	Print Preview	Displays an onscreen preview of how the current project will look on paper.
	Check Spelling	Checks the spelling of text within your project; select a text box to check the spelling of the text contained within.
	Cut	Cuts the selected text or graphic. (Use the Paste command to insert the cut element in a different location.)

continues

Table 2.2   File Toolbar Commands Continued

Button	Name	Function
	Copy	Makes a copy of the selected text or graphic. (Use the Paste command to insert a copy of the selected element in a different location.)
	Paste	Pastes the most-recently cut or copied element to the selected location.
	Undo	Undoes the most-recent action. (You can undo the last several actions by clicking this button several times.)
	Redo	Redoes the last undone action.
	Help	Displays the PrintMaster Help window.
	Art & More Store	Displays the Art & More Store window, which previews graphics that you can obtain from PrintMaster's Online Art Gallery.
	Browse Animated Greetings	Lets you browse through the 3D Animated Greetings you can send via email.
	Photo Organizer	Launches the tool that helps you organize and manage your personal photographs.

The *Format* toolbar is the second (bottom) toolbar at the top of the Design Workspace. The buttons on this toolbar are used to format individual elements within your project. Table 2.3 details the buttons on the Format toolbar, and what they do.

Table 2.3   Format Toolbar Commands

Button	Name	Function
Imperial	Font	Changes font for selected text; pull down the list to select a font.
36	Size	Changes font size for selected text; pull down the list to select a font size, in points.
B	Bold	Boldfaces selected text.
I	Italic	Italicizes selected text.

Button	Name	Function
U	Underline	Underlines selected text.
	Text Shape	Applies a different shape to text in a selected text box; click this button to choose from 32 different text shapes, or click None to display text normally.
	Text Stretch	Stretches text to fill the entire selected text box.
	Left Aligned	Aligns selected text flush left.
	Centered	Centers selected text.
	Right Aligned	Aligns selected text flush right.
	Justified	Justifies selected text.
	Forward One	Moves selected element one layer closer to the top of the "stack."
	Back One	Moves selected element one layer closer to the bottom of the "stack."
	Mirror	Displays a "mirror image" of the selected element.
	Flip	"Flips" the selected element from top to bottom.

The *Edit* toolbar is displayed on the left side of the Design Workspace. The buttons on this toolbar are used to add or modify individual elements within your project, often by launching one of PrintMaster's auxiliary tools. Table 2.4 details the buttons on the Edit toolbar, and what they do.

Table 2.4   Edit Toolbar Commands

Button	Name	Function
	Art	Launches PrintMaster's Art Gallery, where you can select from all available graphics.
	Sentiments	Launches PrintMaster's Sentiment Gallery, where you can select from hundreds of quotes and phrases.
	Cartoon-O-Matic	Launches the Cartoon-O-Matic tool, which lets you create unique cartoon faces.

continues

21

Table 2.4   Edit Toolbar Commands Continued

Button	Name	Function
	Photo Workshop	Launches the Photo Workshop tool, which lets you edit and enhance your personal photographs.
	DrawPlus	Launches the DrawPlus tool, which lets you create and edit drawings and graphics.
	BorderPlus	Launches the BorderPlus tool, which lets you add and edit your project's borders.
	Year You Were Born	Launches the Year You Were Born tool, which adds historic information about a specific date/year to your project.
	Table	Adds a table to your project.
	Headline	Adds a Ready-Made or Custom headline to your project; when the Create a Headline window appears, enter your headline text and select from a variety of styles.
	Custom Graphic	Adds a seal or a timepiece to your project.
	Text Box	Adds a text box to your project.
	Fill Color	Fills the selected element with the chosen color.
	Line	Lets you draw a line within your project.
	Line Format	Lets you change the thickness and color of the selected line.
	Crop	Changes the size of the window containing a picture, effectively "cutting" the edges of the picture.
	Shadow Format	Adds a drop shadow to the selected element.
	Rectangle	Lets you draw a rectangle or square within your project.
	Ellipse	Lets you draw an ellipse or circle within your project.
	Free Draw	Lets you perform freehand drawing within your project.
	Shape	Lets you add a specific shape or symbol to your project.

The Workspace Status Bar

The status bar is located at the bottom of the Design Workspace, and displays information about selected elements, as shown in Figure 2.2. Select an element within your project, and the status of that element is displayed in the status bar.

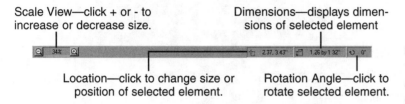

Scale View—click + or - to increase or decrease size.

Dimensions—displays dimensions of selected element

Location—click to change size or position of selected element.

Rotation Angle—click to rotate selected element.

FIG. 2.2

You can view the status of certain elements and make changes to them through PrintMaster's status bar.

Beyond displaying the status of specific elements, you can *change* the status of a selected element by clicking individual parts of the status bar. For example, to rotate an element, select the element in the Design Workspace, and then click in the Rotation Angle section of the status bar; when the pop-up menu appears, select the desired rotation.

Many users don't know that you can use the status bar to change element settings. If you know how to use the status bar in this way, you are already a step ahead!

The Hub

Although PrintMaster's Design Workspace is always present, the first thing you actually see onscreen when PrintMaster launches is the *Hub*. The Hub, shown in Figure 2.3, is where you start all your PrintMaster projects. Just click a button on the Hub to launch a new project, or to access the Art Gallery or the Internet. (If you need to open a preexisting project, close the Hub, pull down the File menu, select Open, and then choose a project from the Project Gallery.)

While the Hub is present, you can't access the Design Workspace; you have to close the Hub to access the Workspace (including any of PrintMaster's menus or toolbars). To close the Hub, click the Cancel button; to redisplay the Hub, click the Hub button on the File toolbar.

Table 2.5 describes all the functions available from the Hub.

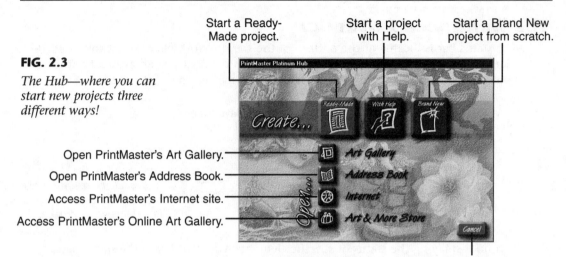

FIG. 2.3

The Hub—where you can start new projects three different ways!

Start a Ready-Made project.

Start a project with Help.

Start a Brand New project from scratch.

Open PrintMaster's Art Gallery.

Open PrintMaster's Address Book.

Access PrintMaster's Internet site.

Access PrintMaster's Online Art Gallery.

Close the Hub and return to the Design Workspace.

Table 2.5   Functions in the Hub

Button	Name	Function
	Ready-Made	Creates a new Ready-Made project with templates from the Project Gallery.
	With Help	Creates a new project using the With Help Designer.
	Brand New	Creates a new blank project.
	Art Gallery	Opens PrintMaster's massive Art Gallery.
	Address Book	Opens PrintMaster's Address Book.
	Internet	Launches an Internet connection and connects to PrintMaster's Internet site.
	Art & More Store	Displays the Art & More Store window, which previews graphics that you can obtain from PrintMaster's Online Art Gallery.

Although there are other ways to start and open projects, the Hub was designed to be the *easiest* way to get started with PrintMaster. If you're like most users, you'll find yourself using the Hub everytime you start a new project.

Workspace Views

When you're working on a project in the Design Workspace, you can choose how large you want that project displayed onscreen. For example, you might want to see the project at its real size; or a *100% view*. Or, you might want to fit the entire project into the Workspace—a *Fit in Window view*.

To change the onscreen size of your project, pull down the View menu and select the desired view. You can choose one of the preselected views, or select the Percent View option to size the project to a 25%, 50%, 100%, 200%, or 400% view.

Another way to change the view of a project is to use the Scale View section of PrintMaster's status bar. You can click the + or - buttons to enlarge or shrink the size of the project, or click the center of the Scale View section to display a pop-up menu containing the same options as on the View menu.

Creating and Editing PrintMaster Projects

Any item you create with PrintMaster is called a *project*. Projects can be greeting cards, banners, newsletters, letterhead, crafts, or even Web pages; if you can create it, it's a project!

You should follow three general steps to work on any PrintMaster project:

1. Pick a project. You can open an existing project, select from one of PrintMaster's premade projects, or create a completely new project from scratch.

2. Add or modify elements. Every project is composed of one or more *elements*; elements can be either text or graphics. You can add new elements to your project, or edit or delete existing elements.

3. Print it—or post it! After your project is completed, you print it out—on your own printer, or (via floppy disk) on a printer at a commercial print shop, such as Kinko's. With PrintMaster 8.0, you can even *post* your project to the Internet as a Web page!

Creating a New Project

You can create a project with PrintMaster in three ways, which are all accessible from the Hub, and all discussed in Chapter 3, "Create, Save, and Reopen PrintMaster Projects."

➤ **Ready-Made.** This is the easiest way to start a new project. When you click the Ready-Made button in the Hub, you open the Project Gallery, where you can select from thousands of predesigned projects. You can then edit these projects to your personal tastes and to include your personal information. You don't have to worry about design issues; because the project is ready-made, it's already been designed for you!

➤ **With Help.** This is another easy way to start a project. When you click the With Help button in the Hub, PrintMaster's With Help Designer launches and guides you step-by-step through the design of your new project. Just answer the onscreen questions and follow the prompts, and you'll end up with a personalized project—quickly and easily!

➤ **Brand New.** If you want to build your project completely from scratch, this is the way to go. When you click the Brand New button in the Hub, PrintMaster's New Project Wizard helps you choose which kind of project you want, and what kind of layout it should have. After that, you're on your own—with all of PrintMaster's tools at your disposal, of course!

How should you start your new project? If you want a good-looking project fast—without a lot of work or customization—choose the Ready-Made option. If you want a personalized project but you don't have a lot of design expertise, choose the With Help option. If you want a completely customized project—and are comfortable with your design skills—choose the Brand New option.

Editing a Project

After you've started a project, you can return to it as often as you want. To open an existing project, just select the File menu and choose Open. When the Project Gallery appears, go to the Project Collection list and select Your Own; all your personal projects appear in the Category section. Just select the project you want to open, and then click the Select button to open the project.

After the project is open, you have a plethora of options available to you. You can add new elements to the project by clicking the appropriate toolbar button or selecting a specific menu option. You can delete any element by selecting the element and then pressing the Delete key on your keyboard. You can even modify an element in any number of ways, including

➤ Resize the element.

➤ Crop the sides of the element.

➤ Change the position of the element on the page.

➤ Rotate the element.

➤ Flip the element top to bottom.

➤ Create a mirror image of the element, left to right.

➤ Layer the element on the page, moving it "up" or "down" in relation to other elements.

➤ Fill the element with color.

➤ Change the thickness or color of the line around the element.

➤ Add a shadow to the element.

All these modifications are accessible through toolbar buttons (most are on the Edit toolbar) and through menu options (most are on the Format menu). In addition, if you select an element and then click your *right* mouse button, you display a pop-up menu with options applicable to the selected element. Note, however, that whatever modification method you use, not all modifications are possible with all elements.

Not Sure What to Choose? Use the Mouse!

If you're not sure what options are available for a particular type of element, just use the right mouse button to display the context-sensitive pop-up menu. This menu automatically displays all the options for the selected element, so you won't have to guess!

Setting PrintMaster's Preferences

There are several aspects to the PrintMaster program that you can customize to your own personal liking. You access these configuration settings from the Preferences dialog box; pull down the File menu and select Preferences. When the Preferences dialog box appears, select the tab containing the preferences you want to change, make the changes, and then click OK.

Table 2.6 details the settings you can change in the Preferences dialog box.

Table 2.6 PrintMaster Preferences

Tab	Preferences
Sound Effects	Select On to play sounds when you perform selected operations; select Off to turn off the sounds.
Help	Check Helpful Hints to display pop-up program hints; check Design Tips to display pop-up design tips; check Play Voice to play voice instructions. (*Uncheck* any options to turn it off.) Click Reset All Hints to recycle previously viewed hints and tips.
Workspace	Increase the Workspace size to make PrintMaster run faster (but use more hard disk space); decrease the Workspace size to conserve disk space.
Date	Pull down the Date Format list to select how PrintMaster displays dates in your projects.

In addition to the options in the Preferences dialog box, you can also tell PrintMaster how to connect to the Internet. Just pull down the File menu and select Online Preferences; when the Online dialog box appears, select whether you're connecting via a modem (and which dial-up connection you're using) or via a direct connection. Click OK when done.

How to Get Help

Although PrintMaster is easy to use, there might be times when you can't figure out a particular operation, or when the program itself starts acting up. Fortunately, a number of different help resources are available.

Within the program itself, you can access PrintMaster's Help system by clicking the Help button in the Design Workspace, or by pulling down the Help menu and selecting Show Help Window. You can browse through the Help topics by selecting the Contents tab, or search for specific Help topics by selecting the Index tab.

In addition, PrintMaster periodically offers pop-up windows with helpful hints and design tips. These include Helpful Hints (suggesting better and more efficient ways to use PrintMaster) and Design Tips (providing professional design advice). If you aren't seeing these pop-up hints and tips, pull down the Help menu and check Show Helpful Hints and Show Design Tips.

Outside the program, you can access official PrintMaster technical support through the following means:

➤ On the web, at www.learningco.com

➤ Via email, at help@tlcsupport.com

➤ Via postal mail, at The Learning Company, 1700 Progress Drive, P.O. Box 100, Hiawatha, IA 52233-0100, Attn: PrintMaster

➤ Via fax, at 319-395-9600

➤ Via phone (automated system), at 800-409-1497

➤ Via phone (live), at 319-247-3333 (between 8:00 a.m. and 8:00 p.m. CST, Monday through Friday)

In the Next Chapter...

Now that you know your way around the PrintMaster desktop, let's find out how to create new projects. Turn to Chapter 3, "Create, Save, and Reopen PrintMaster Projects," to learn more.

Create, Save, and Reopen PrintMaster Projects

Now that you know how PrintMaster works, let's find out how to create your own PrintMaster projects. After you learn how to create a new project, you'll discover how to save your work—and reopen it when you want to work on it some more.

Three Ways to Create a New Project

There are actually three ways to create a new project with PrintMaster, all accessible from the Hub:

➤ **Ready-Made.** This option lets you open one of PrintMaster's several thousand premade projects—and then edit it for your personal needs.

➤ **With Help.** This option employs the With Help Designer, a special "wizard" that leads you step-by-step through the creation of a new project.

➤ **Brand New.** This option is for users who want to do everything themselves— and start with a blank page for their new projects.

Option 1: Creating a Ready-Made Project

The easiest way to create a new project is to start with one that PrintMaster has already made for you! PrintMaster contains thousands of ready-made projects that you can either print as is, or edit with your own personal information and to your own personal tastes.

To create a ready-made project, first go to PrintMaster's Hub. From the Hub, click the Ready-Made button to display the Project Gallery.

Open the Hub

If the Hub isn't open on your desktop, click the Hub button on the File toolbar.

When the Project Gallery appears (see Figure 3.1), choose a ready-made project to open. Although you can scroll through all the thousands of PrintMaster's ready-made projects (just use the scroll bar at the right of the window), it's easier to search for specific types of projects. The Project Gallery lets you search by the following criteria:

Search by collection   Select a project

FIG. 3.1

Search for ready-made projects in the Project Gallery.

Search by project type

Search by category

Search by tone

Search by keyword

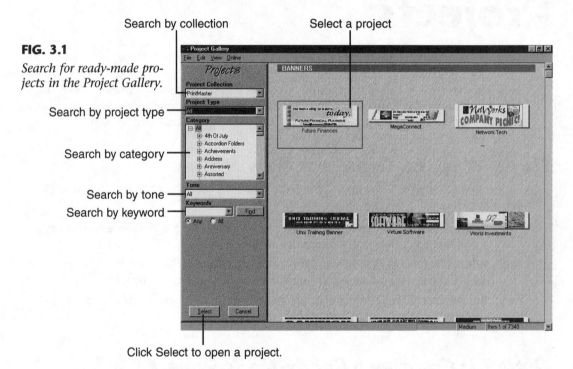

Click Select to open a project.

➤ **Collection.** Pull down the Collection list to choose from a number of project collections, including Your Own, PrintMaster, Craft Corner, and Platinum.

➤ **Type.** Pull down the Type list to choose from different types of projects, from Banners and Brochures & Flyers to Posters and Web Pages.

➤ **Category.** Pull down the Category list to choose from different categories of projects, such as Business, Education, Events, Home, Occasions, and Sports. Click the "+" sign next to any category to see a variety of subcategories.

➤ **Tone.** Pull down the Tone list to choose from a number of different "moods" for your project, such as Humorous, Sentimental, Traditional, Contemporary, and Spiritual.

➤ **Keywords.** Enter one or more keywords to search for specific types of projects. If you want the project to match all your keywords, check All; if you want to match *any* keyword, check Any. Click the Find button to initiate your search.

Use the scrollbars to scroll through matching projects. When you find the project you want to open, highlight it and click the Select button. The ready-made project you selected now appears in a window in the Design Workspace. You can now edit the project to suit your own personal needs.

Insert a CD

Because many projects are stored on additional CD–ROM discs, you might be asked to insert another CD when you select a project. For this reason, keep all your PrintMaster CDs handy—you'll probably need them!

Option 2: Creating a Project with the With Help Designer

If you want more flexibility when creating a project, use PrintMaster's With Help Designer. This feature is a wizard that leads you step-by-step through creating your project so that it looks exactly the way you want it.

To launch the With Help Designer, go to PrintMaster's Hub and click the With Help button. The With Help Designer asks you a number of questions to help you create your perfect project. Depending on how you answer the questions, you'll be led down a path unique to the type of project you want to create.

When the first screen of the Designer appears (see Figure 3.2), select the type of project you want to create. Then, follow the Designer as it asks you project-specific questions, as described in the following list:

➤ **Calendar.** You are asked whether you want a monthly, weekly, or yearly calendar; when you want your calendar to start (and how many periods you want it to cover); whether you want a picture on your calendar (and whether you want the picture on the top or the side); whether you want a Business, Educational, or Personal calendar; and which style of calendar (within your chosen category) you want.

➤ **Greeting Card.** You are asked to specify the type of card you want to create (Anniversary, Birthday, Holiday, Romantic, or Invitation); the type of recipient, holiday, or category for your card; the style for your card; and the recipient's name.

➤ **Label.** You are asked which kind of label you want to create (Address, Diskette, Name Badges, or Shipping); the type of label you will be printing to; the style for your labels (Business, Educational, or Professional); the design style within your overall style (Classical, Contemporary, or Whimsical); and whether you want to print the same text on all labels, insert names from your Address Book, or print blank labels.

➤ **Letterhead.** You are asked to determine the type of letterhead you want to create (Business, Floral, or Personal); a style for your letterhead; and your name and address to personalize the letterhead.

➤ **Newsletter.** You are asked to specify the category for your newsletter (Business, Educational, or Personal); the style (Classical, Contemporary, or Whimsical); the length in pages; and whether it is double-sided.

➤ **Poster.** You are asked to specify the category of poster you want to create (Event, For Sale, Home, Kid Stuff); what type of poster you want; and the information you want displayed on your poster.

➤ **Web Page.** You are asked to determine the category of Web page you want to create (Business, Community, Personal), and the style for your page (Classic, Contemporary, Whimsical).

FIG. 3.2

Use the With Help Designer to select what type of project you want to create.

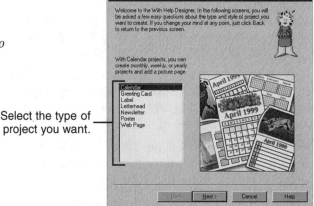

Select the type of project you want.

When the Designer is done asking questions, it creates a project (to your specs) in the Design Workspace, ready for your fine-tuning.

Option 3: Creating a Brand-New Project

If you want complete control over your project, you should skip both the ready-made projects and the With Help Designer. What you really want is the PrintMaster equivalent of a "blank slate," where you can add any elements you choose using a design you create from scratch. To create a totally unique project, use PrintMaster's Brand New option—and then start creating!

Actually you can start a brand-new project in two ways:

➤ Choose the File menu and select New.

➤ Click the Brand New button on the PrintMaster Hub. (If the Hub isn't open on your desktop, click the Hub button on the File toolbar.)

Taking either of these actions opens the New Project window, shown in Figure 3.3. This window lets you choose from a number of different types of projects, including

FIG. 3.3

Selecting any option in the New Project window opens a blank project of the selected type.

➤ Blank Page (select this option to create a project that doesn't fit within established categories)

➤ Poster

➤ Quarter-fold Card

➤ Half-fold Card

➤ Banner

➤ Calendar

➤ Label

➤ Envelope

➤ Business Card

➤ Certificate

➤ Note Card

➤ Fax Cover

➤ Letterhead

➤ Newsletter

➤ Brochure

➤ Web Page

➤ Post Card

➤ Sticker

➤ T-Shirt

➤ Craft

➤ Easy Prints

Selecting a specific type of project gives you a little head start on your project (mainly in terms of project dimensions and onscreen options). However, if you want a completely blank slate, select the Blank Page option.

After you've made a selection, click the Next button. For most types of projects you are asked the project's orientation (tall or wide) or dimensions. Make the appropriate selections and then click the Finish button. PrintMaster opens a new project window in your Design Workspace containing a blank project sized to your specifications—and ready for any element you choose to add.

Editing Your Projects

When your new project appears in the Design Workspace, you can select any element of the project to edit, including

➤ Background (see Chapter 6, "Better Backgrounds")

➤ Lines and drawings (see Chapter 7, "Better Lines and Drawings")

➤ Pictures and photographs (see Chapter 8, "Better Pictures and Photographs")

➤ Text (see Chapter 9, "Better Text")

You can also add new elements to your project, or delete any existing elements. In short, you can change anything in the project to make it truly your own.

Save Your Project

After you've selected your project, you should save it—and then you should resave it after any substantial edits.

To save a project for the first time, follow these steps:

1. From the Design Workspace, choose the File menu and select Save As.
2. When the Save As dialog box appears, select *where* you want to save the project from the Save In list or by using the file management buttons. Then, name the project by entering a name in the File Name box.
3. Select a project type from the Save As Type list.
4. If you want to add this project to the Project Gallery, check the Add to Project Gallery option and select a category from the Category list—or click the New button to create a new project category.
5. After you've made your selections, click the Save button to save this new project under the filename you selected.

Don't Overwrite a Ready-Made Project!

Remember to save any new ready-made project under a *different name,* using the Save As command. If you make changes to a ready-made project and then click the Save button (instead of selecting Save As), you'll save your version of the project under the ready-made project filename—which means the original ready-made project won't exist anymore! It's a good idea to use the Save As command to rename your project as soon as you open it to protect against over-writing the ready-made project.

After your project has been initially saved (and named), it's much easier to save subsequent versions of your file. Just click the Save button on the File toolbar (or pull down the File menu and select Save) and your project is saved, quickly and easily.

Reopening a Previous Project

Few projects are completed in one session. Quite often you'll want to return to a project to make some changes and adjustments—or just to print out additional copies.

To open a preexisting project, follow these steps:

1. From the Design Workspace, choose the File menu and select Open. (Alternately, click Ready-Made from the Hub.)
2. When the Project Gallery appears, select Your Own from the Project Collection list.
3. Scroll through the gallery of projects you've created until you find the project you want to open; highlight that project, and click the Select button.

PrintMaster File Formats

Each type of project created by PrintMaster is saved in a unique file format. You can look for these different file types on your hard disk, using My Computer or Windows Explorer:

Type of Project	File Type
Banners	BAN
Brochures	BRO
Business cards	BIZ
Calendars	CAL
Cards	CAR
Certificates	CER
Envelopes	ENV
Fax covers	FAX
Half-fold cards	HCR
Labels	LBL
Letterhead	LET
Newsletters	NWS
Note cards	NOT
Postcards	PCR
Posters	SIG
Stickers	STI
T-shirts	TSH
Web pages	WEB

In the Next Chapter...

When your project is finalized, you'll want to print it. To learn how to print with PrintMaster, turn to Chapter 4, "Print Your Projects."

Print Your Projects

After you've finished a project, you'll want to print it, which you can do from your standard computer printer. If you're printing a color project, you'll need a color printer; color projects just don't look right in black and white! And if the output from your printer isn't high enough quality, take your project to a service bureau for professional printing.

Read this chapter to learn all about the *best* ways to print your PrintMaster projects!

Configuring Your Printer in Windows

Before you print your project, you should be sure that PrintMaster is configured properly for your particular printer.

The basic settings for your printer are configured via standard Windows operations—and differ, to a degree, depending on your individual printer. You access your specific printer's configuration by choosing PrintMaster's File menu and selecting Print Setup. When the Print Setup dialog box appears, select the printer you want to use from the Name list, confirm the size and source of your paper, and select either Portrait (standard) or Landscape (sideways) orientation. You can click the Properties button to configure more advanced settings for your particular printer; otherwise, click OK to save these settings.

Printing a Normal Project

When it comes time to print a particular project, you need to confirm a few settings before you actually start your printing. When you click the Print button on the File toolbar (or choose the File menu and select Print), you see the Print dialog box, shown in Figure 4.1.

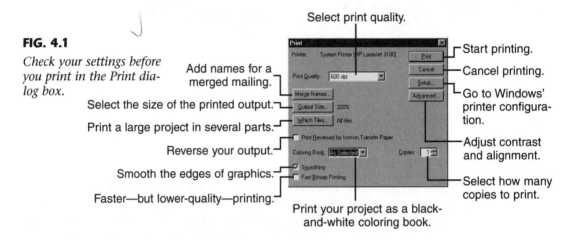

FIG. 4.1

Check your settings before you print in the Print dialog box.

Select print quality.

Start printing.

Cancel printing.

Go to Windows' printer configuration.

Add names for a merged mailing.

Select the size of the printed output.

Print a large project in several parts.

Reverse your output.

Smooth the edges of graphics.

Faster—but lower-quality—printing.

Adjust contrast and alignment.

Select how many copies to print.

Print your project as a black-and-white coloring book.

Make Last-Minute Adjustments

From within the Print dialog box, you can make a number of adjustments to the current print job, including

➤ **Print Quality.** Many printers allow you to print your projects at several different quality levels. (Print quality is called *resolution*, and is sometimes measured in *dots per inch*, or *dpi*; in other cases, printers may simply have High, Medium, or Low resolution settings.) Select an output resolution from the Print Quality list. Note that lower resolutions print faster but may look rough; higher resolutions take longer to print, but look more professional. Use lower resolutions for "draft" outputs, and the highest possible resolution for your final printout.

➤ **Merge Names.** If you're producing a merged mailing (discussed in Chapter 10, "Better Projects with PrintMaster's Special Tools"), click this button to select the names to include from your Address Book.

➤ **Output Size.** You can print your project at any size; normal size is 100%. When you click the Output Size button you see the Custom Print Size dialog box; you can specify how many inches or sheets tall or wide you want your project to print, or you can specify the *scale* (measured as percent of the original) of your output. You may want to use this option to print smaller versions of your project for proofing purposes.

➤ **Which Tiles.** Large projects have to print on multiple sheets of paper; for printing purposes, each printed page is called a *tile*. When you click the Which Tiles button, you see the Tiles to Print dialog box; select which tiles of your project you want to print. (Normally, you'll want to print the entire project, so click Turn All On and then click OK.)

➤ **Coloring Book.** PrintMaster lets you print most types of pictures as a black-and-white outline, much the way a coloring book looks (before it's colored in, that is!). To print your entire project as a coloring book, select All from the Coloring Book list; to print only selected graphics in black-and-white outline, highlight those elements of your project and then select As Selected from the Coloring Book list.

➤ **Smoothing.** If you've included low-resolution bitmapped graphics in your project (or overly enlarged a very small graphic), check the Smoothing option to "smooth" the rough edges of the graphics.

➤ **Fast Bitmap Printing.** When "proofing" a project, you want fast output, and you don't need to see your project exactly as it will look in its final output. When you check Fast Bitmap Printing, all the graphics in your project print in black and white, which is faster than standard color printing.

➤ **Print.** Click this button to initiate printing.

➤ **Cancel.** Click this button to cancel the current print job.

➤ **Setup.** Click this button to open Windows' printer setup dialog box and adjust specific printer settings.

➤ **Advanced.** Click this button to adjust the contrast and alignment of your project (see the next section for more details).

➤ **Copies.** Click the up or down arrow to increase or decrease the number of copies of this project you want to print.

After everything is set properly, click the Print button to start printing. You can cancel your print job at any time by clicking the Cancel button.

Printing in Black and White?

If you're going to be printing your final project on a black-and-white printer, you should design your project in black and white. Although PrintMaster will try to convert color elements to grayscale for black-and-white printers, the conversion isn't always perfect. You're better off editing each project element to change all the colors to black, white, or tones of gray—that way, you know how your project will look *before* you print it.

Adjusting Advanced Settings

If your printed output doesn't look quite right, you can adjust some advanced settings to make things look a little better on paper. When you click the Advanced button in the Print dialog box, the Advanced Settings dialog box appears as shown in Figure 4.2.

FIG. 4.2

You can adjust PrintMaster's advanced print settings in the Advanced Settings dialog box.

You can adjust the following from the Advanced Settings dialog box:

➤ **Outline Picture Contrast.** Use this slider to adjust the contrast of printed images from CGM and WMF files. Adjust the slider to the left for lighter printing, and to the right for darker printing.

➤ **Bitmap Picture Contrast.** Use this slider to adjust the contrast of printed images from GIF, JPG, TIF, PCX, and BMP files.

What Are All These Formats?

To learn more about the various picture formats (CGM, GIF, JPG, and so on), turn to Chapter 8, "Better Pictures and Photographs."

➤ **Print As Bitmap.** Check this option to print a picture in black and white.

➤ **Print Alignment.** Click this button (or choose the File menu and select Print Alignment) to reposition your project on paper. When the Printer Alignment dialog box appears, follow the onscreen directions to print a test page and then enter critical measurements in the proper boxes. This helps PrintMaster adjust its output to the specifics of your individual printer.

Preview Your Printout

Before you actually print your project, you probably want to preview—onscreen—what your printed output will look like. To do this, either click the Print Preview button in the File toolbar, or choose the File menu and select Print Preview.

As you can see in Figure 4.3, a preview of the print job appears in the Design Workspace. Click the Zoom In and Zoom Out buttons to see more or less of the printout; click Prev Page and Next Page to preview multiple-page projects. You can initiate actual printing by clicking the Print button, or click the Close button to end the preview without printing.

FIG. 4.3

Previewing your printing—click Print to print what you see.

Printing a Special Project

Although most projects print as described, some types of projects have special printing needs. Let's look at a few of the special types of printing you might encounter while using PrintMaster.

Print a Single Picture Multiple Times—On a Single Page

PrintMaster has a special printing option called Easy Prints that lets you print several copies of a picture (or any PrintMaster element) on a single page, in a variety of sizes. (These are sometimes called *thumbnails*.) Easy Prints is a good way to preview how your pictures will look when printed at different sizes.

To create an Easy Print, go to the Hub and click the Brand New button. When the New Project dialog box appears, select Easy Prints and click Next. When the Choose a Photo Project Type dialog box appears, select one of the photo layouts, and then click Finish.

You'll now be taken to the Design Workspace, which is currently blank (and waiting for you to insert the picture you want to print). Click the Art Gallery button and select the picture you want to print; that picture appears in the Design Workspace. (Note that the picture in the Workspace does *not* represent the photo layout you chose earlier.) Click either Print Preview to preview your multi-image printout, or Print to begin printing.

Print Multiple Pictures in a Catalog

PrintMaster also lets you print a *catalog* of different pictures (great for reference use). Just go to the Art Gallery or Project Gallery, choose the File menu, and select Print. When the Print Art dialog box appears, select whether you want to print the selected picture (Print Selected Picture), print the current page of pictures (Print Current Picture), or print all pictures in this gallery (Print All Pictures). Then, select how many pictures you want to display on each page (anywhere from 2 to 48 per page), confirm your normal print settings, and click the Print button to start printing.

Print Pictures As a Coloring Book

You can use PrintMaster to make a "coloring book" out of your pictures. This prints the pictures as outlines only, with all colors replaced by white. To print a project as a coloring book, go to the Print dialog box, and select All from the Coloring Book list.

Print Iron-On Transfers

To make an iron-on transfer out of your project (great for ironing on T-shirts!), you need to print a mirror image of your project. (Don't forget to put iron-on transfer paper in your printer, of course.) Just go to the Print dialog box and check the Print Reversed for Iron-On Transfer Paper option; PrintMaster sends the image reversed to your printer.

Print Postcards, Business Cards, and Labels

If you're printing postcards, business cards, or labels, a few additional print options are available to you.

To be sure PrintMaster knows which type of postcard you're printing to, choose the Edit menu and select Postcard Type. When the Choose the Postcard Size dialog box appears, select the type of postcard you're printing to and click OK.

You have a similar configuration to make if you're printing labels or business cards. Choose the Edit menu and select Label Type. When the Choose a Label Type dialog box appears, check either Laser or Dot Matrix labels, and then select the type of label or card you're printing to—and be sure the preview box looks like the labels/cards you have. Click OK when you're done selecting.

In addition to these settings, the Print dialog box contains a few extra settings when you're printing cards and labels:

➤ **Number of Labels/Card.** Enter the total number of cards or labels that you'll be printing.

➤ **Starting Label/Card.** Specify which card or label (on the first sheet of cards or labels) you'll be starting with. (This is useful when you're printing on a partially used sheet of cards or labels.)

➤ **Print Range (postcards only).** Because postcards are two-sided items, you can choose to print Both Sides, the Front Only, or the Back Only.

➤ **Double-Sided (postcards only).** Check this box to print on both sides of your postcard.

Print Envelopes

Printing envelopes is a little more complicated than printing other types of projects. In addition to the normal print settings, you must select which names to print on your envelopes (by using the Mail Merge feature, discussed in Chapter 10, "Better Projects with PrintMaster's Special Tools"), as well as *how* to print the envelopes on your printer.

To configure your envelope feed, click the Envelope Feed button. Select how your envelopes are fed into your printer (Flap Up or Flap Down, Rotated or Reverse Landscape), and then click one of the six different orientations that best matches your printer. (When in doubt, just click the Default button—it works most of the time.) Click OK when done.

Print Double-Sided Projects

Some projects are two-sided, and need to print on both sides of a sheet of paper. To configure PrintMaster for double-sided printing of a specific project, choose the File menu and select Double-Sided Print Setup.

When the Double-Sided Printing Wizard appears, follow the onscreen directions to print and compare a series of test pages. After you tell the wizard how the tests stack up on your printer, it then configures PrintMaster to print the pages in the correct sequence for your particular setup.

Print Large Projects

If your project is too large to fit on a single sheet of 8.5-×11-inch paper (such as a banner or a very large card), PrintMaster offers several options.

First, you can simply resize the output to print on a single sheet. To do this, go to the Print dialog box and click the Output Size button. When the Custom Print Size dialog box appears, select a new size for your printed output, either in inches wide/tall, sheets wide/tall, or scale (percent of the original size).

Second, you can choose to print a large project in multiple tiles; you then assemble the separate tiles to create your finished project. PrintMaster automatically breaks up large projects into smaller tiles for printing. If you want to print only selected tiles, go to the Print dialog box and select Which Tiles; when the Tiles to Print dialog box appears, click the individual tiles that you want to print, or select Turn All On to print all tiles.

Printing with an Outside Print Service

If you don't want to print your project on your own printer, you can use an outside print service (such as Kinko's or PIP Printing) to do your printing for you. To do this, you have to find a print service that has PrintMaster installed on its computers. After you confirm that your print service can handle PrintMaster files, use My Computer or Windows Explorer to make a copy of your project file to a floppy disk, and then take that floppy disk to your print service. It will then open your project on its copy of PrintMaster, and send it to one of its printers to print.

In the Next Chapter...

In this first section, you've learned a number of PrintMaster basics, including essential program operations and how to print a project. To build really cool projects, however, you need to know how to add and edit the elements that comprise your projects. So start learning how to build your PrintMaster projects in Chapter 5, "Better Designs."

PART 2

Get Productive: How to Build Better Projects

Better Designs

All PrintMaster projects start with a blank page. Various *elements* are placed on top of that page, layered one on top of another, to create your finished project. PrintMaster includes various types of elements, from text to shapes to clip art to photographs; each element has its own unique characteristics that you can edit for best effect. All elements, however, share some basic characteristics, and this chapter shows you—in general terms—how to work with all the elements you use in your PrintMaster projects.

Add a New Page

Most projects start with a single page. To add a new page to certain types of projects (such as newsletters or brochures), choose the Add menu and select Pages. When the Add Pages dialog box appears, enter the Number of pages to add and whether you want the new page(s) to appear After or Before the current page. You can also choose to add blank pages, or a copy of the current page. Click OK to add the page(s).

Working with Elements

Anything you add to your project—a picture, a shape, a text box, you name it—is, by definition, an element. Most elements can be added by clicking the appropriate button in the Edit toolbar or selecting an option from the Add menu.

To make changes to an element, you first have to select the element in the Design Workspace. There are several ways to select an element:

➤ Click the element with your mouse. To select multiple elements at the same time, hold down the Shift key while clicking the elements.

➤ Position your cursor in a blank area of the Design Workspace and then click and hold your mouse button. Drag the cursor over the element(s) you want to select until the selection box completely surrounds the element(s).

➤ Press Tab to cycle through all the elements in your project one at a time; press Shift+Tab to cycle backward through the elements. (This method might be the only way for you to select an element that is completely layered beneath one or more other elements.)

After the element is selected, *selection handles* (those little black boxes shown in Figure 5.1) appear around the element. You can then use any of PrintMaster's tools to edit the appearance of the element.

FIG. 5.1

Drag a selection handle to resize an element; drag the rotation handle to rotate the element.

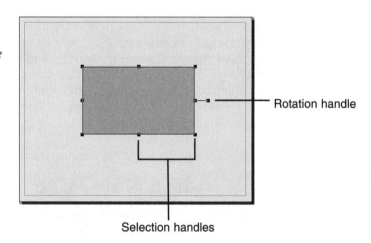

Rotation handle

Selection handles

Use the Pop-Up Menu

To display a list of relevant tools for editing the selected element, just select the element and click your *right* mouse button. A pop-up menu appears containing the editing commands pertaining to the selected element.

Take It Back!

If you make a change to an element that you shouldn't have made, click the Undo button on the File toolbar (or choose the File menu and select Undo). Click this button several times to undo multiple actions.

Group Multiple Elements

For some specific tasks, you might want multiple elements to behave as if they were one single element. When elements are grouped, you can move or resize all of them with a single action.

To group elements, hold down the Shift key while selecting them to select multiple elements. After all the elements are selected, choose the Arrange menu, and select Group. Now, all the elements function as a group; any action you take affects the group, not the individual elements. You can, however, *ungroup* a group (and turn the group back into individual elements) by selecting the group, choosing the Arrange menu, and selecting Ungroup.

Create a Border from Duplicate Elements

You can make copies of small elements and group them for borders, headers, footers, or backgrounds. Just select the element you want to duplicate, choose the Edit menu, and select Duplicate. When the Duplicate dialog box appears, choose the arrangement you want (Tiled Header, Tiled Footer, Staggered, Tiled Border, or Tiled Cover), and then click OK. Your duplicated elements are automatically grouped as a single element; when you move or resize one, you move or resize them all.

Move the Element

It's relatively easy to move an element. Just select the element, and then position your cursor somewhere over the element. (Your cursor changes shape, from a simple arrow to a four-sided arrow.) Click and hold your right mouse button and drag the element to its new position; release the mouse button when you have the element where you want it.

You can also use the arrow keys on your keyboard to move a selected element up, down, right, or left. Pressing two adjacent arrow keys together (such as up and right) moves the element diagonally.

More Precise Positioning

To learn how to position your elements precisely in the Design Workspace, see the "Arranging Your Elements" section later in this chapter.

Resize the Element

To resize an element easily, use your mouse to "grab" any of the element's selection handles, and then drag the handle until the element reaches its desired size. If you drag a top or side handle, you resize the element only vertically or horizontally; if you drag a corner handle, you resize the element in both directions.

Be careful when you resize an element; it's easy to change the element's proportions when you resize just one dimension of the element. To maintain the element's original proportions during resizing, hold down the Shift key while dragging one of the selection handles. When you do this, the element is resized equally in both the vertical and horizontal dimensions.

To size the element to a precise measurement, select the element, choose the Arrange menu, select Position, and then select More. When the Confirm dialog box appears, select the Size tab. You can set the element's height or width as a percent of the page, or enter precise measurements (in inches) for the element's height or width. (Note that changing both height and width changes the element's proportions.) Click OK to make your changes.

Resize for Uniformity

PrintMaster allows you to select multiple elements and resize them so that they have the same width or height. Use the Shift key to select the multiple elements simultaneously, and then choose the Arrange menu, select Position, and then select More. When the Confirm dialog box appears, select the Relative tab. In the Size section, select Shrink to Smallest to match the width or height to the smallest selected element; select Grow to Largest to match the width or height to the largest selected element.

Twi

1 to 360 degrees. The easiest
dle and drag the element around
ent reaches its desired rotation.
down the Shift key while drag-

ct and then click the rotation
e one of the preselected rotations,
g box—where you can specify the

Fli

ld look better facing right, or one
ng down. Fortunately, PrintMaster

ge menu and select Flip Top to
eft to right), choose the Arrange
hen you mirror an element, any
ard—just as it would when viewed
g and mirroring an element.

FIG. 5.2
You can flip and mirror an element.

ent

ent
bottom

ent
o right

Fil

, or a Picture

color, almost all elements can be
or. In fact, you can fill many ele-
ns (also called *blends*), patterns
s.

What You Can Fill—And What You Can't

Any shape (rectangles, ellipses, and so on) can be filled with solid colors, blends, textures, and graphics. Text and photos can be filled only with solid colors. When you open the Color Palettes dialog box, only those fill options available for the selected element appear; you won't be presented with an option that you can't apply.

To recolor an element, select the element and then click the Fill Color button on the Edit toolbar (or choose the Format menu and select Fill Color). When the Color Palette dialog box appears, you have several options, depending on the type of element you're trying to recolor. (Not all elements let you fill with blends, textures, or photos; if these options are not available, their tabs will not be visible.) See Table 5.1 for the types of coloring options available; see Figure 5.3 for examples of each type of fill.

Text or Text Box?

If you're recoloring text, highlight all the letters/words you want to recolor; do *not* select the entire text box. If you select the entire text box, you'll be filling the entire box with color.

Table 5.1   Fill Options in the Color Palette Dialog Box

Type of Fill	Follow These Instructions
Solid color	Select the Color tab (if available). Click the color you want to use. To see additional colors, click the More button and when the Colors dialog box appears, click the Define Custom Colors button and choose a new color.
Color blend (gradation)	Select the Color tab (if available). Click the starting color for the blend, the blend style, the blend angle, and the desired blend pattern.
Texture (pattern)	Select the Texture tab (if available). Click the desired pattern; use the scrollbar to view more patterns. To make the pattern lighter, pull down the Tint list and select a lesser percentage.

Type of Fill	Follow These Instructions
Photo	Select the Photo tab (if available). Click the Import button to select a graphics file. Click the Edit button to use Photo Workshop to change the picture. Pull down the Tint list and select a lower percentage to make the picture lighter.

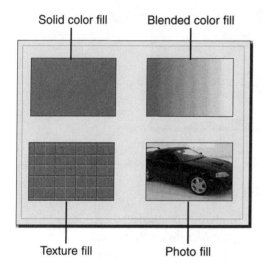

Solid color fill   Blended color fill

Texture fill   Photo fill

FIG. 5.3

Examples of PrintMaster's different types of fills.

To realize the full impact of PrintMaster's fill option, you need to experiment with different types of fills. Try filling an object with a solid color, a blend, a texture, and a photo—and use the Undo command to cancel any fills you don't like!

Add a Shadow

PrintMaster can add a shadow to any element in your project, including shapes, lines, pictures, and text. Shadows add depth to your elements—almost like the element was raised a tad off the page. To add a shadow, just select the element and then click the Shadow Format button. When the pop-up menu appears, select the direction of the shadow (Drop Down Right, Drop Down Left, Drop Up Right, Drop Up Left), click the Color button, and select the shadow's color.

Crop to Fit

Sometimes, you have a picture or other graphic where the point of interest occupies only part of the entire picture. Instead of putting up with a lot of graphic dead space,

PrintMaster lets you *crop* part of the element out of the picture—thus, effectively eliminating parts of the picture you don't want to see. Figure 5.4 shows a picture pre- and post-cropping.

FIG. 5.4

You can crop the edges of a picture.

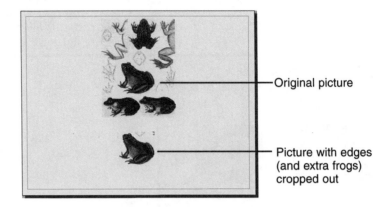

Original picture

Picture with edges (and extra frogs) cropped out

Cropping Isn't Permanent

When you crop a picture in PrintMaster, you change only the way it looks within this particular project. The original picture continues to exist, uncropped. In fact, you can return to the element at any time and change the cropping to show parts of the picture you may have previously cropped.

Follow these steps to crop the edges of an element:

1. Select the picture you want to crop.
2. Click the Crop button on the Edit toolbar (or choose the Format menu and select Crop).
3. Place the cursor over one of the element's selection handles; the cursor should change to resemble the shape on the Crop button.
4. Drag the selection handle inward to crop that edge of the picture.
5. Alternately, place the cursor over the center of the picture; the cursor should change into a hand shape. Click and hold the mouse button and drag the picture within the window; if you drag any part of the picture beyond the edge of the window, that part of the picture is effectively cropped from view.

Crop and Enlarge

You might want to crop a picture to emphasize a smaller aspect within the larger picture. Just cropping the edges of the picture might not accomplish the desired effect; you might also need to enlarge the remaining part of the picture, effectively filling a larger space with a smaller component.

Arranging Your Elements

Although you can drag elements around the Design Workspace, there are times you'll need more precise positioning. PrintMaster provides several ways to position your elements automatically, eliminating the need to "eyeball" the final placement.

Align with Rulers and Guides

PrintMaster includes several positioning elements to help you guide the position of your elements.

First, the Design Workspace includes both horizontal and vertical *rulers*, along the top and left sides of the project window. Use the rulers to position your elements on the page.

Can't See Your Guides or Rulers?

If no guides are visible in your Design Workspace, choose the View menu and check Guides. If no rulers are visible, choose the View menu and select Rulers.

Second, PrintMaster enables you to set *guides* for more precise positioning. These guides are blue horizontal or vertical lines that help you move elements to a precise position.

To add a guide to your project, move your cursor to a specific point on either the horizontal or vertical ruler, and then click the left mouse button. After a guide is created, you can use your mouse to drag it to a new position, if desired. You can lock any guide in position by choosing the Arrange menu and selecting Lock Guides. To remove a guide, drag it back to the ruler.

Snap Your Guides to the Ruler

To set a guide at an exact position, choose the Arrange menu and select Snap to Rulers. When this option is selected, any guides you create automatically "snap" to the 1/4-inch marks on the vertical and horizontal rulers. (Deselecting Snap to Rulers lets you position guides between the 1/4-inch marks.)

After you've created a guide, you can make nearby elements "snap" to a guide's position. (For this feature to work, choose the Arrange menu and check Snap to Guides.) When Snap to Guides is activated, any element you move near a guide automatically positions itself on the guide.

Position Relatively

PrintMaster supplies commands that let you automatically center an element on your page—either horizontally, vertically, or absolutely. Just select the element, choose the Arrange menu, select Position, and then select one of the following options:

➤ **Center on Page.** This option positions the center of the element in the absolute center of your project's page.

➤ **Center Horizontally.** This option centers the element horizontally (left to right), without changing the element's vertical position.

➤ **Center Vertically.** This option centers the element vertically (top to bottom), without changing the element's horizontal position.

➤ **Full Page.** This option centers the element absolutely and then stretches it to fill the entire page.

➤ **More.** This option lets you precisely position the element anywhere on the page; see the next section for more details.

Position Precisely

Sometimes—particularly on professional print jobs—you need to position an element *precisely* on the page. PrintMaster enables you to specify the specific position of any element, in both the vertical and horizontal dimensions.

Begin by selecting the element, choose the Arrange menu, select Position, and then select More. When the Confirm dialog box appears, select the Position tab, and select either Left, Center, or Right for Horizontal alignment, and Top, Middle, or Bottom for Vertical alignment. Enter a distance in the At boxes to represent the space from the edge of the page to the selected part of the element (Left, Right, Top, Center, and so on). If you want to center the element, check Space Equally.

For example, if you want the edges of your element to be 2 inches in from the left and 1 1/2 inches down from the top, check Left and enter **2 in.** for the Horizontal alignment, and check Top and enter **1.5 in.** for the Vertical alignment. Click OK to reposition the element.

Align Multiple Elements

If you have multiple elements on your page, you can have PrintMaster align them in a neat and precise pattern. Just select all the elements you want to align, choose the Arrange menu, select Position, and then select More. When the Confirm dialog box appears, click the Relative tab. (This tab appears only when multiple elements are selected.)

From here, you can choose to line up all the selected elements along their left or right edges, their top or bottom edges, or their horizontal or vertical centers. (Note that selecting Centers for both horizontal and vertical effectively places the elements directly on top of each other.) You can also change the *size* of the selected elements, growing them all to the size of the largest element or shrinking them all to the size of the smallest element. Click OK when done.

Stack in Layers

In PrintMaster's Design Workspace, multiple elements are effectively "stacked" on top of each other in layers; any element on an upper layer covers an element on a lower layer. Layers are created when you add new elements to your project—when you add a new element, you add a new layer, as well. (Figure 5.5 shows several elements layered on a page.)

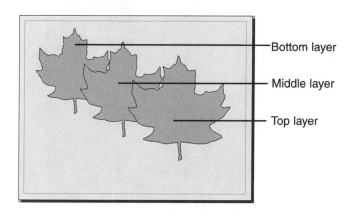

Bottom layer

Middle layer

Top layer

FIG. 5.5

Three elements layered on top of each other; elements on top obscure elements on lower layers.

Sometimes, an element at the bottom of your stack needs to be moved to the top of the stack to be visible; other times, an element at the top needs to be at the bottom, to serve as a background. To move an element up or down through the stack of layers, select the element, choose the Arrange menu, select Layer, and then select one of the following options:

➤ **Bring to Front.** This option moves the selected element all the way to the top of the stack.

➤ **Forward One Layer.** This option moves the selected element one layer higher in the stack.

➤ **Back One Layer.** This option moves the selected element one layer lower in the stack.

➤ **Send to Back.** This option moves the selected element all the way to the bottom of the stack.

Create a Matching Set

Many real-world projects involve more than one item. If you're preparing for a birthday party, for example, you may need to create birthday cards, invitations, banners, name tags, posters, and thank-you notes. If you're creating a new business identity, you may need business cards, letterhead, envelopes, fax cover sheets, and brochures. In all instances, you want each piece to look identical to the other pieces.

Although you could use PrintMaster to create each piece separately and *hope* you get the designs close enough to pass, there is a better way to establish a uniform identity across multiple related pieces. PrintMaster lets you create *Matching Sets*, where different projects share the same look and feel automatically. As you can see in Figure 5.6, the projects in a Matching set share the same color scheme, theme, and graphics—and are easy to create.

FIG. 5.6

Different projects, same look and feel—the various elements of a Matching Set.

To create a Matching Set, follow these steps:

1. Go to the Hub and click the Ready-Made button.
2. When the Project Gallery appears, choose the Project Type list and select Matching Sets; all projects within a Matching Set appear grouped.
3. Select projects within the Matching Set, one project at a time.

Each project within a matching set appears in its own project window. You can now work on each project separately.

Changes Aren't Universal!

When you change a graphic in one Matching Set project, the graphic changes automatically in the other projects. However, if you change any other aspect of the design in one project, the other projects do *not* automatically change—you'll need to change each project separately!

In the Next Chapter...

This chapter has shown you how to work with PrintMaster elements, in general terms. Now, let's look at how you can work with specific types of elements to create stunning effects in your projects. Start with the backgrounds for your projects; turn to Chapter 6, "Better Backgrounds" to learn more.

Better Backgrounds

If you create a project from scratch, you start with a blank—and very white—page. Although many items look good with a white background, you can make a more interesting project by adding a more interesting background.

In PrintMaster, a project's background is just another element. In particular, the background is a shape that has been moved to the bottom layer in your project.

A project's background can be a single color, a gradated blend of colors, a texture/pattern, or even a photograph or graphic. Just browse through PrintMaster's ready-made Project Gallery to see how backgrounds are used to enliven a variety of different projects.

How to Add a Background

If you want a plain white background for your project, you don't have to do anything—that's the default background for any PrintMaster project. If you want anything other than a white background, however, you have to add a shape (typically a rectangle) to the bottom level of your project; that shape will be your new background.

To add a background shape to a project:

1. Open your project, choose the View menu, and select Fit in Window.
2. Click the Rectangle button in the Edit toolbar (or choose the Add button menu and select Rectangle).
3. Draw a rectangle that covers the entire page of your project.
4. To make sure the rectangle really does cover the entire page, select the rectangle, choose the Arrange menu, and select Full Page.

5. Send the rectangle to the bottom of your stack of elements by selecting it, choosing the Arrange menu, selecting Layer, and then selecting Send to Back. (If the background is the first element you add to a new project, you don't have this option—the first element added is automatically the bottommost layer of your project.)

Now that you've added a background layer to your project, you can add different types of fills to the element—effectively creating different types of backgrounds.

Use a Background As a Cover Page

If you create a really cool background, it doesn't have to stay in the background! If you're producing a multiple-page project—such as a report—use your background as the project's cover page. This is especially interesting if the background has been lightened by shading or tinting it; create a version of the background *without* the shading/tinting to use as a full-color front cover!

Creating Color Backgrounds

It's easy to fill your background element with color. In fact, you can fill it with either a solid color (see Figure 6.1) or a gradated blend of colors, as shown in Figure 6.2. (A gradation blends two colors—typically black or white with a third, user-selected color—in a user-selected fill pattern.)

FIG. 6.1

A single-color background—in this case, a dark background with lighter foreground elements.

Here is the text for this example.

FIG. 6.2

A gradated background—dark on top (behind the headline) and lighter on the bottom (behind the graphic).

Contrast Counts

For optimal readability, you need a strong contrast between text and background. Don't put light text on a light background, or dark text on a dark background—always put light on dark, or dark on light. The best readability is black text on a white background, as boring as that may sometimes seem.

Be careful when using a gradated background, especially if the color gradation is from a very dark color to a very light color. Placing lighter elements on the dark part of the background, and darker elements on the light part of the background can get tricky. Also tricky are those elements that bridge the light and dark parts of the gradation. For this reason, you're better off using less-extreme gradations for your backgrounds so that all elements can be placed anywhere on the background without viewability problems.

To fill your background element with a solid or blended color, follow these steps:

1. Select your background element.
2. Click the Fill Color button on the Edit toolbar (or choose the Format menu and select Fill Color).
3. When the Color Palette dialog box appears (see Figure 6.3), select the Color tab.

FIG. 6.3

Changing the background color with the Color Palette dialog box.

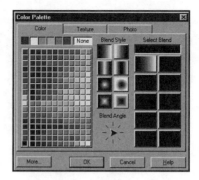

4. To fill the element with a single color, click a color, and then select the top (solid) option in the Select Blend section.

Make Your Own Colors

To select from colors not displayed in the Color Palette dialog box, click the More button. When the Color dialog box appears, click the Define Custom Colors button. When the dialog box expands, click anywhere on the color rainbow to select a new color, move the slider up and down to lighten or darken the chosen color, and then click the Add to Custom Colors button. Click the OK button to return to the Color Palette dialog box; your new color is chosen.

5. To fill the element with a color blend, click the color you want to use as your starting color. Select a Blend Style, as well as a Blend Angle. Now, select one of the blends in the Select a Blend section (which blends your selected color with other preselected colors), and then click OK.

Reversed Text Is Hard to Read

Although a strong contrast between text and background helps text to stand out, *reversing* text (using light text on a dark background—white against black, for example) can be tiring on the eyes, especially at smaller text sizes. Reverse text is great for headlines and limited areas, but creating an entire document of small reverse type is asking way too much of the reader.

Creating Patterned Backgrounds

PrintMaster lets you create a background composed from a graphic pattern—what PrintMaster calls a *texture*. When you choose a pattern (which is just a small graphic or photograph), that pattern is repeated over and over again to create a full background, as shown in Figure 6.4.

FIG. 6.4

A patterned background—simple, yet effective.

Keep It Simple

A background that is too "busy" (too much detail, too many elements, and so on) can make it hard to read anything sitting on top of the background. This is especially a problem when you have small text on a busy background. Your options are to choose a simpler background, or use only larger text and graphics. A busy background with large white text works fine for a headline; however, for the body of a document (with smaller text), a busy background can make the text unreadable.

To fill your background element with a repeating pattern, follow these steps:

1. Select your background element.
2. Click the Fill Color button on the Edit toolbar (or choose the Format menu and select Fill Color).
3. When the Color Palette dialog box appears, select the Texture tab.
4. Scroll through the available textures until you find the one you want; click it to select it.

5. If you want to lighten the pattern, pull down the Tint list and select a lesser percentage.

6. Click OK to apply the pattern to your background.

More Backgrounds—Online

A number of Web sites offer background graphics, either free or for a fee. The first (and most obvious) to visit is PrintMaster's Online Art Gallery. To preview the art available online, go to the Hub and click the Art & More Store button.

Other sites offering a wide variety of interesting backgrounds include

➤ Art Today (www.arttoday.com)

➤ Barry's Clip Art Server (www.barrysclipart.com)

➤ ClipArtConnection (www.clipartconnection.com)

➤ ClipArtNow (www.clipartnow.com)

➤ MediaBuilder (www.mediabuilder.com)

➤ Netscape Background Sampler (www.netscape.com/assist/ net_sites/bg/backgrounds.html)

➤ Texture Land (www.meat.com/textures/)

Follow the instructions at each site to download the graphics to your computer. In addition, any background you can use for a Web page or the Windows desktop can also be used as background for a PrintMaster project.

Creating Graphic and Photographic Backgrounds

Perhaps the most sophisticated backgrounds are composed of photographs or other types of graphics. PrintMaster includes a large number of clip art and photographic elements ideal for background use in its Art Gallery; however, you can use any type of photograph or graphic file as a background.

FIG. 6.5

A photographic background—great for large projects, such as posters or banners.

Lighten Up!

Whether you're using a graphic or a pattern as a background, you can create a more sophisticated—and easier-to-read—effect by lightening the background element. You do this by selecting a percentage from the Tint list in the Color Palette dialog box; a 20%–30% tint is generally good to start with.

Note that if you try to duplicate a lightened image (with a 20% tint, let's say), the duplicate image will be a lightened version of the original lightened image (20% of 20%, in our example). If you want the duplicate to retain the same tint percentage as the original, you'll have to go back to the Color Palette dialog box and change the Tint to 100%.

To fill your background element with a user-supplied graphic, follow these steps:

1. Select your background element.
2. Click the Fill Color button on the Edit toolbar (or choose the Format menu and select Fill Color).
3. When the Color Palette dialog box appears, select the Photo tab.
4. Click the Import button, and browse your hard disk for a specific graphics file.
5. To edit the imported graphic or photograph with PrintMaster's Photo Workshop, click the Edit button.
6. To make the graphic lighter, pull down the Tint list and select a lesser percentage.
7. Click OK to fill the background element with the graphic image.

If you want to use one of PrintMaster's graphics as your project's background, the procedure is a bit different. First off, you *don't* want to create a rectangle and then fill it with a file; instead, you can just add the graphic itself to your project, and send it to the background layer.

Follow these steps to use a PrintMaster graphic as a background layer:

1. With a blank project open, click the Art Gallery button in the Edit toolbar (or choose the Add menu and select Picture).

2. When the Art Gallery appears, go to the Categories list and select Backgrounds. (Click the "+" next to Backgrounds to view different categories of background images.)

3. Select the background image you want to use, and then click the Select button. (Try to select an image that matches the orientation of your project; select a tall image for a portrait orientation, or a long image for a landscape orientation.)

4. PrintMaster places your selected image in the Design Workspace; you now have to resize to fill the entire project background. Do this by selecting the element, choosing the Arrange menu, selecting Position, and then selecting Full Page.

5. Make sure the graphic is sent to the back of your project by selecting the element, pulling down the Arrange menu, selecting Layer, and then selecting Send to Back. (If this graphic is the first element you add to a new project, you don't have this option—the first element added is automatically the bottommost layer of your project.)

Recolor Your Graphic to Make It Lighter

If the graphic you added is too dominant, you can recolor it to appear lighter in the background. Just select the element, click the Fill Color button, and select a light color from the Color Palette dialog box. Some form of light gray generally provides a good lightening effect.

Creating Complex Backgrounds

For certain types of projects, you may want to have a different background behind certain elements. For example, in a newsletter, you may want a plain white background behind the majority of the page, but a color or photographic background behind a special column.

Although there are a number of ways to do this, the easiest is to fill the selected text box with your color, texture, or photograph of choice. Alternately, you create a new rectangular object (filled appropriately) and position it directly behind your selected area—one layer down, of course.

How to Group Multiple Elements

To group multiple elements, select them all simultaneously (by holding down the Shift key while selecting them), choose the Arrange menu, and then select Group. The grouped elements now function as a single element, which can be sent to the back of the stack.

Multiple Pages, Multiple Backgrounds

If your project has multiple pages, you'll need to copy your background to each additional page. (This is another good reason to group multiple background elements—it gives you just one thing to copy.) Of course, you could choose to have different backgrounds on different pages, but that typically is confusing, and not recommended.

Creating Borders with BorderPlus

In addition to creating backgrounds for your projects, you can also frame your projects with borders. There are actually three ways to add a border to a PrintMaster project:

➤ **Use a graphic image for your background that includes a border.** PrintMaster's Art Gallery has many such "border" backgrounds; open the Art Gallery, go to the Categories list, and select Borders to display the graphics.

➤ **Use multiple graphic images to construct a border manually.** Any graphic sized properly and repeated around the edge of a page can create a border. In fact, many of the images in the Art Gallery's Borders section are actually *parts* of borders (corners, straight lines, and so on); add these multiple graphics to your project, group them, and then send them to the bottom layer.

➤ **Use BorderPlus.** This last option is the most interesting one. BorderPlus is an add-on tool that creates either shaded or graphic borders for your PrintMaster projects. It's easy to use, and provides spectacular results.

To create a border with BorderPlus, follow these steps:

1. From within an open project, click the BorderPlus button on the Edit toolbar, or choose the Add menu and select Border.

2. Use your cursor to draw a rectangle describing the size and position of your border. (Most of the time this means outlining the entire page of your project; to do this, you'll need to use the Fit In Window view to display your entire project onscreen.)

3. When you finish drawing your border and release the mouse button, the BorderPlus window appears, as shown in Figure 6.6. Your border is shown in eight segments: top, bottom, left, right, top-right corner, top-left corner, bottom-right corner, and bottom-left corner.

FIG. 6.6

Use BorderPlus to frame your project with a border.

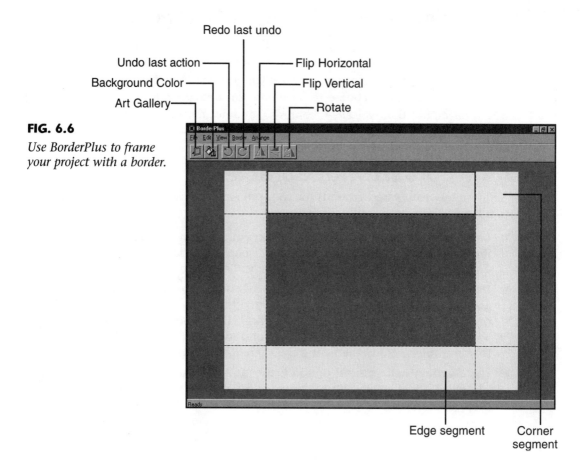

4. To resize the width of the border, position your cursor over an inside edge, hold down your mouse button, and drag the border in or out. (When you resize one side, the other side automatically resizes; when you resize the top or bottom, the other one automatically resizes, also.)

5. To create a color border, click the Background Color button, and then select a color from the Color Palette dialog box.

6. To add a graphic to any one of the border segments, select the border segment and then click the Art Gallery button. When the Art Gallery appears, go to the Category list, select Borders, and then select an appropriate border graphic for that segment of the border.

Add All Sides—Or Corners—At One Time

To insert the same graphic into all sides or all corners of your border, choose the BorderPlus' Border menu and select either Select Edges, Select Corners, or Select All—and *then* click the Art Gallery button to select a graphic. All segments that are selected receive the chosen graphic.

A quicker way to copy and rotate corner elements automatically is to insert the first corner graphic (typically in the top-left corner), select that corner segment, choose the Arrange menu, and then select Copy to Corners. This command automatically copies the graphic to all four corners and rotates it accordingly. (The Copy to Edges option performs a similar function for edge graphics; the Copy Across option copies and rotates a graphic from side to side or top to bottom.)

7. If you need to rotate a graphic within a border segment (which you might need to do with some corner graphics), select the segment and then click the Rotate button until the graphic is angled correctly. (You can also Flip a graphic horizontally or vertically, using the appropriate buttons on the BorderPlus button bar.)

8. When your graphic is completed, choose the File menu and select Done Editing Border; your new border is automatically inserted into your project.

Remember to use the Layer command to send your border to the background of your project. If you need to edit an existing border, just double-click the border to reopen the BorderPlus window for your border.

FIG. 6.7

*A fancy border, created
with BorderPlus.*

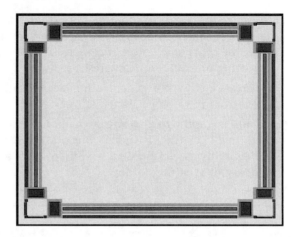

In the Next Chapter...

Now that you know how to create interesting backgrounds and borders, let's put
some elements on top of your backgrounds. To start with the simplest types of elements, turn to Chapter 7, "Better Lines and Drawings."

Better Lines and Drawings

Now that you have a background for your project, it's time to add some elements to the foreground. In this chapter, you'll learn how to add lines, shapes, and drawings to your PrintMaster projects, using a variety of tools.

Adding Lines

Adding a line to your project is simple. Start by clicking the Line button in the Edit toolbar (or choosing the Add menu and selecting Line) and positioning your cursor where you want the line to start. Then, click and hold the mouse button while you drag the cursor over the path of the line, and release the mouse button when you come to the end of the line. You can edit a preexisting line by selecting the line and then dragging one or both of the end handles to a new position.

To draw a line at a perfect 45-degree angle (perfectly horizontal, vertical, or diagonal), hold down the Shift key while you're drawing the line or moving the preexisting line handles.

Rules Are Good

A perfectly horizontal line—otherwise known as a horizontal *rule*—is a great way to break up or separate different sections of a large or complex project.

Change the Width and Color of Your Lines

By default, PrintMaster draws a black line with hairline width. If you want a thicker or different color line, just select the line and click the Line Format button (or choose the Format button and select Line). When the pop-up menu appears (as shown in Figure 7.1), select a new line width (from hairline to 8 pts.); if you want a custom line width, click the More button and enter the desired width in the Line Width dialog box.

FIG. 7.1

Click the Line Format button to change the width and color of a preexisting line.

To change the color of a line, click the Line Format button and then click the Color button on the pop-up menu. When the Color Palette dialog box appears, select the color for the line—when you click the color, the dialog box automatically closes and your line changes to the new color.

A Different Kind of Line

If you want a thicker line with texture or pattern, don't draw a line—draw a long, thin rectangle. Then, you can fill the rectangle with a texture or picture, for a really interesting effect.

Draw Complex Lines with Free Draw

If you like drawing—or want something more complex than just a straight line—use PrintMaster's Free Draw function. This function lets you draw on the page just as you would with a pencil and paper.

From your open project window, click the Free Draw button (or choose the Add menu and select Free Draw). Position your cursor where you want to start drawing, and then click and hold the mouse button. As long as you hold down the mouse button, you're drawing on your page—lines, curves, whatever you want.

When you release the mouse button, whatever you've drawn becomes a single element within your project, as shown in Figure 7.2. You can resize, move, or rotate the entire element; click the Line Format button to change the width or color of the line you drew; click the Shadow Format button to add a shadow to your drawing; or click the Fill Color button to add a color, pattern, or picture to the "spaces" between your lines.

FIG. 7.2

A freehand drawing created with Free Draw; below it is a copy with the "spaces" filled with color and a shadow added.

Just What Are You Filling?

Use the Fill Color function carefully on elements created with the Free Draw function. The results are somewhat unpredictable, because the program tries to figure out just what is "inside" and what is "outside" your lines. If you draw something that doesn't have a clear inside and outside, figuring out the inside versus the outside isn't always easy to do!

Adding Simple Shapes

You could use the Free Draw function to draw a rectangle or circle by hand, but unless you're really talented, the results might be less than acceptable. Instead, use PrintMaster's built-in functions to add perfect premade shapes to your projects. See Figure 7.3 to see some of the shapes you can create.

FIG. 7.3

Some of PrintMaster's shapes—a rectangle filled with a color blend, an ellipse filled with a texture, and a shape filled with a photograph.

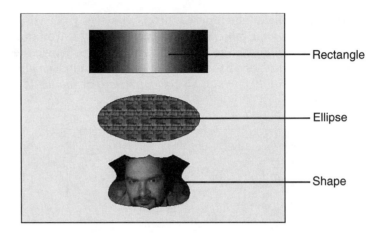

Rectangle

Ellipse

Shape

Rectangles and Squares

To add a rectangle to your project, select the Rectangle button on the Edit toolbar (or choose the Add menu and select Rectangle). Then, position your cursor where you want to place one corner of the rectangle, and click and hold the mouse button while you draw the rectangle on your page. Release the mouse button to finalize your rectangle. To draw a square, hold down the Shift key while you're using the Rectangle tool.

You can edit a preexisting rectangle by selecting the object and then dragging one of the selection handles to a new position. Change the width or color of the rectangle's border by clicking the Line Format button; select a different line width from the pop-up menu, or click the Color button to select a new color from the Color Palette.

To fill your rectangle with a different color, texture, or picture, select the rectangle and click the Fill Color button. When the Color Palette dialog box appears, select the Color tab to add a solid color or color blend; select the Texture tab to add a patterned fill; or select the Photo tab to fill the rectangle with a picture.

You can also add a shadow to your rectangle by clicking the Shadow Format button on the Edit toolbar and choosing the type and color of shadow desired.

Draw a Diamond

A diamond is just a square on its corner. Hold down the Shift key while using the Rectangle tool to draw a perfect square. Then, grab the square's rotation handle and (holding down the Shift key again) rotate the square a perfect 45 degrees. Voilà! You've just drawn a diamond!

Ellipses and Circles

To add an ellipse to your project, select the Ellipse button on the Edit toolbar (or choose the Add menu and select Ellipse). Then, position your cursor where you want to place one corner of the ellipse, and click and hold the mouse button while you draw the ellipse on your page. Release the mouse button to finalize your ellipse. To draw a perfect circle, hold down the Shift key while you're using the Ellipse tool.

You can edit a preexisting ellipse by selecting the object and then dragging one of the selection handles to a new position. Change the width or color of the ellipse's border by clicking the Line Format button; select a different line width from the pop-up menu, or click the Color button to select a new color from the Color Palette.

To fill your ellipse with a different color, texture, or picture, select the ellipse and click the Fill Color button. When the Color Palette dialog box appears, select the Color tab to add a solid color or color blend; select the Texture tab to add a patterned fill; or select the Photo tab to fill the rectangle with a picture.

You can also add a shadow to your ellipse by clicking the Shadow Format button on the Edit toolbar and choosing the type and color of shadow desired.

Shadow, No Border

Default objects are created with a hard black border that doesn't always look natural. You can achieve a more sophisticated effect by removing the border (click the Line Format button and select None) and adding a gray drop shadow to the object (click the Shadow Format button, select Drop Down Right, and then click the Color button and select a medium gray color).

Other PrintMaster Shapes

In addition to round and rectangular shapes, PrintMaster includes several other pre-drawn shapes you can add to your projects. When you click the Shape button on the Edit toolbar (or choose the Add menu and select Shape), you display the Shapes palette, shown in Figure 7.4. Select a shape from this palette (or click the More button to see even more shapes), and then use your cursor to place and size the shape on your page. (Hold down the Shift key while drawing to maintain the shape's original dimensions.)

FIG. 7.4

Add a predrawn shape to your project from the Shapes palette; click the More button to see even more shapes.

As with rectangles and ellipses, you can change the width and color of the shape's border; click the Fill Colors button to fill the shape with a color, texture, or picture; or click the Shadow Format button to add a shadow to the object.

Vector Versus Bitmap

The shapes you create with PrintMaster's shape commands—as well as the pictures you create in DrawPlus—are called *vector* graphics. Vector graphics are images that are created via geometrical formulas; they can be resized and stretched and still maintain their original resolution and smooth edges. In contrast, *bitmap* graphics (such as those created in Photo Workshop) are created via a pattern of dots, and become "blockier" when enlarged. (Note that all scanned photographs, as well as JPG and GIF files, are bitmap graphics.)

Adding and Editing Sophisticated Drawings with DrawPlus

In addition to PrintMaster's simple shape functions, the program also includes a sophisticated drawing/editing tool called *DrawPlus*. With DrawPlus, you can create your own drawings and artwork, or edit PrintMaster's premade graphics.

DrawPlus on the Web

DrawPlus is a vector-based graphics/illustration/drawing program developed by Serif, Inc. Access Serif's Web site (www.serif.com) to learn about its other useful products, such as PagePlus (a desktop publishing program), PhotoPlus (a photo-editing program), and other graphics-oriented software programs.

There are two ways to launch DrawPlus:

➤ From within PrintMaster, click the DrawPlus button on the Edit toolbar (or choose the Add menu and select Drawing Object).

➤ Launch DrawPlus independent of PrintMaster by clicking Windows' Start menu, selecting Programs, and then choosing Serif DrawPlus.

DrawPlus is a full-featured program with a variety of tools and functions. Figure 7.5 shows the main DrawPlus window, with some of the more important tools highlighted.

Standard toolbar—shortcuts
to common functions

Toolbar—select tools for
creating and editing objects.

Editing toolbar—
format text and lines.

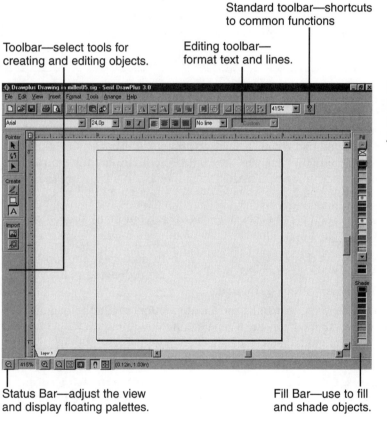

FIG. 7.5

Use DrawPlus to create sophisticated drawings and graphics.

Status Bar—adjust the view
and display floating palettes.

Fill Bar—use to fill
and shade objects.

Why Should You Use DrawPlus?

In earlier versions of PrintMaster, DrawPlus added picture-editing functions that weren't found in the main PrintMaster program. As PrintMaster has become more robust over time and multiple versions, its built-in picture-editing functions have come to rival those of DrawPlus. In many cases, you can create the pictures you want within PrintMaster without ever launching the DrawPlus tool; in other cases, you'll need a slightly more sophisticated effect that PrintMaster doesn't offer, so you'll need to use DrawPlus. It's good to have the option available.

Creating and Modifying Pictures

When you launch DrawPlus, it opens with a blank picture displayed. You can begin drawing on this picture, or you can create a new picture by clicking the New button on the Standard toolbar. When you click the New button, you display the Startup Wizard; click Start from Scratch to open a blank picture, or Open a Drawing to open an existing picture.

DrawPlus lets you add several different types of elements to your blank page, including

> **Lines and curves.** Click the top button in the Create section of the toolbar, and then select either Freehand Tool (for totally freehand drawing), Line Tool (for straight lines), or Curve Tool (for curves).

> **Shapes.** Click the QuickBox button in the Create section of the toolbar, and then select a predrawn shape from the Shape Palette.

> **Text.** Click the Text Tool button in the Create section of the toolbar to add floating text to your picture.

> **Imported pictures.** Click the Import Picture button on the toolbar to display the Import Picture Wizard; use the wizard to import a picture from a Photo CD, Scanner, or other source.

> **Graphics from the Art Gallery.** Click the Insert Picture button on the toolbar to select a picture from PrintMaster's Art Gallery.

Elements that you add to your DrawPlus pictures can be edited in a variety of ways. You can resize and reposition them using the Selection Tool (the first button in the Pointer section of the toolbar); you can rotate them using the Rotate Tool (second button in the Pointer section); you can fill the object with various colors and shades and blends with options on the Fill Bar; and you can perform a variety of flipping, layering, and shadowing functions with options on the Standard Toolbar.

Using Your DrawPlus Pictures

When you're done creating or editing your DrawPlus picture, you can do three things with it:

➤ **Place the picture in your PrintMaster project and close DrawPlus.** To do this, choose the DrawPlus' File menu and select Exit & Return.

➤ **Place the picture in your PrintMaster project and keep DrawPlus open for additional projects.** To do this, choose the DrawPlus' File menu and select Update.

➤ **Save the picture to a file on your hard disk.** To do this, choose the DrawPlus' File menu and select Save Copy As.

You can also print a copy of the picture you created; just choose the DrawPlus' File menu and select Print.

Other DrawPlus File Options

If you launch DrawPlus outside of PrintMaster (from the Windows Start menu), you have different options available for saving your files. Because any pictures you create in this fashion aren't associated with specific PrintMaster projects, you won't see the options for Update, Save Copy As, or Exit & Return. Instead, you see normal Windows file commands: Save and Save As.

In the Next Chapter...

In this chapter, you learned how to draw your own lines and shapes for your PrintMaster projects. In the next chapter, you learn how to work with photographs and preexisting graphics, using PrintMaster's Photo Workshop and Photo Organizer tools. Turn to Chapter 8, "Better Pictures and Photographs," to learn more.

Better Pictures and Photographs

A project with all text—no matter what font you choose—can lack visual interest. People like to look at pictures—especially pictures of people—so adding pictures to your projects can increase their visual appeal.

You can add pictures to your projects in several ways. You can choose from the tens of thousands of graphic images included with PrintMaster; you can import picture and clip-art files from other sources (such as the Internet); or you can use your own personal photographs in digital format. This chapter shows you how to use all these different types of pictures in your PrintMaster projects.

Pick a Picture from PrintMaster's Art Gallery

PrintMaster includes tens of thousands of graphic images you can use in any PrintMaster project. (Different versions of PrintMaster include different numbers of images; PrintMaster Platinum 8.0 has the most of any version, with more than 160,000 images.) These images consist of both *clip art* (nonphotographic images) and photographs.

Not All Pictures Are Free to Use

Just because you have access to a picture (either through PrintMaster or if you find it on a Web site) doesn't mean that you're free to use that picture however you choose. Pictures that are in the *public domain* are free for your use, but many other pictures can be used only for your own personal use—*not* for public or commercial use.

In the case of PrintMaster graphics, PrintMaster owns or licenses all the images available within the program. You may use all PrintMaster graphics to design your own creations, as well as to create items that promote your business, event, or organization—provided that you don't make commercial use of an image as your business, logo, or trademark.

Some PrintMaster images may be incorporated in commercial projects, provided that you're not making money off of the image itself. The images that can be used in this fashion can be identified by searching by the keyword **EULA** in the Art Gallery. (EULA stands for End User License Agreement.) If the word EULA does not appear for a specific image, that image *can't* be used in any commercially distributed products.

If you want to use an image found at a specific Web site, check with that Web site about its usage restrictions. Some sites might limit your use of certain images; some might require a payment or royalty for use of the image; some might require that you include a notice similar to the PrintMaster notice; and others might let you use their images with no restrictions. Just remember—ask permission before you use any image you find on the Web!

Selecting from the Art Gallery

All of PrintMaster's graphic images are contained in the Art Gallery. You open the Art Gallery by selecting the Art Gallery button in the Edit toolbar; by choosing the Add menu and selecting Picture; or by going to the Hub and selecting the Art Gallery button.

As you can see in Figure 8.1, the Art Gallery consists of drawings, photographic images, borders, and paintings. The images are organized by collection and by category, and can also be searched by tone and keyword.

Collection list

Category list

Images

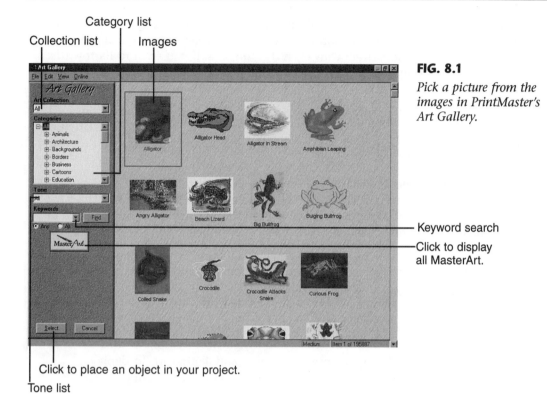

FIG. 8.1

Pick a picture from the images in PrintMaster's Art Gallery.

Keyword search

Click to display all MasterArt.

Click to place an object in your project.

Tone list

You use the following lists and features to find images in the Art Gallery:

➤ **Art Collection.** PrintMaster organizes its artwork into various *collections*. You can choose to display images from All collections, Your Own collection (images you've created and saved), the PrintMaster collection (standard PrintMaster images), and the Online Art Gallery. In some versions of PrintMaster, each Art CD is listed as its own separate collection.

➤ **Categories.** Choose from 28 major categories, from Animals and Architecture to Travel and Western. Click the "+" next to a category to display subcategories.

➤ **Tone.** You can choose to display only those images that reflect a certain mood or tone; choose from Humorous, Sentimental, Traditional, Contemporary, Spiritual, or All.

➤ **Keywords.** You can search for specific types of images by entering a query of one or more words into the Keywords box, choosing whether you want to match Any or All of your keywords, and then clicking the Find button. All images that match your query appear in the art browser window.

For example, if you want to display all humorous PrintMaster images of birds, select PrintMaster from the Art Collection list, select Birds (under Animals) from the Categories list, and select Humorous from the Tone list. If you want to narrow this further to display only images of roosters, enter **rooster** in the Keywords box and click Find.

If you want to view *all* PrintMaster images, select All from the Art Collection, Category, and Tone lists, and choose the Keywords list and select <None>. Use the scrollbar on the right side of the art browser window to scroll through all the matching images.

To select an image and place it in your project, click the image and then click the Select button. If the image is stored on your hard disk, it is immediately placed in your project; if the image resides on one of PrintMaster's Art CDs, you are asked to insert the CD and then the image is copied to your project.

Art from the Masters

In addition to the standard PrintMaster art gallery, PrintMaster includes the *MasterArt Collection* of exclusive images from more than 60 internationally known painters, designers, and illustrators. To display the MasterArt Collection, click the MasterArt button in the Art Gallery.

Going Online for More PrintMaster Art

The PrintMaster box doesn't contain *all* of PrintMaster's art images; even more images are online in PrintMaster's Art & More Store. This Web site provides access to PrintMaster's Online Art Gallery, where you can preview thousands of new drawings and photographs—and download the ones you like!

The artwork in the Online Art Gallery includes these collections:

➤ Bedtime Stories

➤ Fanciful Holidays

➤ Janet Carder

➤ Nostalgic Valentines

➤ Victoriana Christmas and New Year's Eve

Each of these collections provides a handful of free sample graphics, plus an additional 50–100 graphics you can download for a fee.

Follow these steps to find and download images from the Online Art Gallery:

1. From either the Hub or the File toolbar, click the Art & More Store button.

[handwritten: Acct Name ALLEGRINI]
[handwritten: Password Boat]

Register Before You Download

Before you can download anything from the Online Art Gallery (including lists of available images), you need to register with the site. When asked to register, fill in your name, choose a password, and enter your email address—and write down this information for future use. (You can also register ahead of time by going to the Art Gallery, choosing the Online menu, and selecting Create a New Account.)

2. When the Art & More Store window appears as shown in Figure 8.2, browse through the selections; click the Download button to download previews of a collection's contents.

FIG. 8.2

Browse through the collections in the Online Art Gallery.

3. After the previews have been downloaded, click the Preview button to use PrintMaster's Art Gallery to view thumbnail versions of the art in the selected collection.

4. When you click an image, the Available for Purchase dialog box appears. To view the image (and other images in the same set), click the View Set button. To order a specific image, click the Order Form button.

5. The price for the selected image and instructions for ordering appear onscreen. Follow the onscreen instructions to order the image.

6. You'll now receive an "unlock" code to add this image to your current collection.

Editing Your Pictures

After you've selected a PrintMaster graphic, you can perform some simple editing tasks on the picture. (You can also use Photo Workshop—discussed later in this chapter—for more heavy-duty editing.) Here are some of the simple changes you can make to the graphics in your PrintMaster projects:

➤ **Replace a picture.** You can replace any picture you've added to your project with any other picture from the Art Gallery (or any other source). PrintMaster automatically transfers many of the changes you make—such as flipping or mirroring—from the original picture to its replacement. To replace a picture, select the original picture in your project, choose the Edit menu, and select Replace Picture. When the Art Gallery appears, choose a new picture, and click the Select button; the new picture replaces the selected picture. (Note that if the new picture is a different size from the original, you may have to resize it to fit in the same space.)

➤ **Crop a picture.** To crop the edges of a picture, click the Crop tool on the Edit toolbar, grab one of the picture's selection handles, and pull the edge of the picture inward to its new position.

➤ **Recolor a picture.** Most of PrintMaster's built-in images are constructed from dozens—if not *hundreds*—of individual colors. PrintMaster lets you *recolor* the picture by changing the black component of the picture to a different color, effectively casting a different-color tint on the image. To do this, select the picture, click Fill Color in the Edit toolbar (or choose the Format menu and select Fill Color), and then choose a new color from the Color Palette dialog box. (To return a picture to its original tint, repeat this procedure and select black in the Color Palette dialog box.)

➤ **Lighten a picture.** To make a picture appear lighter on the page, select the picture, click Fill Color in the Edit toolbar (or choose the Format menu and select Fill Color), and when the Color Palette dialog box appears, click the More button. When the Color dialog box appears, click the Define Custom Colors button to expand the dialog box, select white as the color, and then move the Tint slider to a light setting. Click OK when done.

If It's in the Background, Lighten It Up

If you're using a graphic as part of your project's background, you may want to lighten it so that it's less intrusive to the main elements you have in the foreground.

Importing Other Graphics Files into PrintMaster

Even though PrintMaster provides over a hundred thousand images, that's just a drop in the ocean to the millions and millions of images available from other sources. If you have an image from another source—from a Web site, or a clip-art disk, or from a scan of a personal photograph—you can *import* that image into PrintMaster and use it as you would any other image.

PrintMaster lets you import graphics in most popular file formats, including those listed in Table 8.1.

Table 8.1   Image Formats Supported by PrintMaster

File Format	Description
BMP	A simple graphics format (stands for "bitmap") that is the default format for Windows desktop backgrounds.
CGM	A vector graphics format (stands for Computer Graphics Metafile).
GIF	A popular Web-based graphics format (pronounced "jif"). GIF files can include transparent backgrounds (so that a Web page background can show through) and can include multiple images for a simple animated effect.
JPG	Another popular Web-based graphics format (pronounced "jay-peg"). JPG files are often slightly smaller in size than comparable GIF files.
PCX	An older graphics format (pronounced "pee-see-ex"), not normally used on Web pages. PCX files can be used as desktop backgrounds for more recent versions of Windows.
PSD	The official file format of Adobe Photoshop.
TIF	A graphics format (pronounced "tif"), not widely used on Web pages. TIF files are popular with professional desktop publishers.
WMF	A file format used for graphics in Windows applications (stands for Windows Metafile Format).
Kodak PhotoCD	A proprietary format for storing digital photographs.

Add a Picture to Your Project

To import a graphics file into your project, go to the Art Gallery, choose the File menu and select Open from Disk. When the Open Picture from Disk dialog box appears, select the picture you want to import, and click OK. The imported picture is placed in the middle of your current project, ready to be moved, resized, or otherwise edited.

Where to Find Artwork on the Internet

Hundreds of Web sites specialize in images of all different types, from bullets and icons to clip art and drawings to high-resolution photographic images. Here are some of the best art sites on the Internet:

➤ Art Today (www.arttoday.com)

➤ Barry's Clip Art Server (www.barrysclipart.com)

➤ ClipArtConnection (www.clipartconnection.com)

➤ ClipArtNow (www.clipartnow.com)

➤ Corbis (www.corbis.com)

➤ Icon Bank (www.iconbank.com)

➤ Mediabuilder (www.mediabuilder.com)

➤ PrintEverything (www.printeverything.com)

➤ Smithsonian Photo Archive (photo2.si.edu)

In addition, several search engines and directories let you scour the Internet for the images you need. Check out these image search sites:

➤ About.com Web Clip Art Links (webclipart.about.com)

➤ AltaVista Photo and Media Finder (image.altavista.com)

➤ Amazing Picture Machine (www.ncrtec.org/picture.htm)

➤ Arthur (www.ahip.getty.edu/arthur/)

➤ Clip Art Review (www.webplaces.com/html/clipart.htm)

➤ Clipart Directory (www.clipart.com)

➤ Lycos Image Gallery (www.lycos.com/picturethis/)

➤ NCrtec Good Photograph and Image Sites (www.ncrtec.org/tools/picture/goodsite.htm)

➤ WebSEEk (www.ctr.columbia.edu/webseek/)

➤ Yahoo! Image Surfer (ipix.yahoo.com)

In addition to these Web sites, tons of Usenet newsgroups specialize in posting images of various types. Although many of these newsgroups are erotic in nature, a large number of general-interest picture newsgroups are also available. Look in the alt.binaries.pictures.* hierarchy for the groups that focus on pictures.

Add a Picture to the Art Gallery

In addition to adding a picture directly to a project, you can also import graphics files and store them in the Art Gallery for use in future projects. To add a picture to the Art Gallery, go to the Art Gallery, choose the File menu, and select Import. When the Open Picture from Disk dialog box appears, select the picture you want to import, check the Make Local Copy of File box, and then click OK. A copy of the file you selected is added to the Your Own Art category in the Art Gallery.

Export a PrintMaster Graphic

PrintMaster lets you import pictures into the program, and it also lets you *export* PrintMaster graphics for use in other programs. To save a PrintMaster graphic to your disk in a format usable by other programs, go the Art Gallery, select the picture you want to export, choose the File menu, and then select Export. When the Export dialog box appears, select a destination for the file and click the Save button. (Note: You can't change the file type for the picture you're saving; pictures must be exported in their original formats.)

Print Plain Pictures—Without Creating a New Project

You don't have to add a picture to a project to print it. To print a plain picture, choose PrintMaster's Tools menu and select Print Pictures from Disk. When the Print Pictures dialog box appears, change to the folder that contains your pictures, select the file(s) you want to print, and then click the Print button. When the Print Picture Catalog dialog box appears, select how many pictures per page you want to print, and click the Print button to begin printing.

Adding Your Own Photographs to a Project

Nothing personalizes a project more than one of your own personal photographs. There are two ways to get your photographs into PrintMaster; you can *scan* an existing picture into a digital file, or you can use a *digital camera* to take your pictures digitally to begin with.

Scan a Photograph

A scanner is a piece of hardware that works much the same way as an office copier; it optically "reads" a picture and then converts (*digitizes*) that image into a digital graphics file that can be used by your computer. Most scanners come with their own software that can save scanned images in a variety of formats; if you're using this software, save your scans in either TIF format (if the ultimate output is a printed page) or JPG format (if the ultimate output is a Web page or email attachment).

In addition to your scanner's proprietary software, PrintMaster includes special TWAIN technology to "acquire" images directly from your scanner (or digital camera). When you use PrintMaster to manage your scanning, your scanned image is placed directly in your PrintMaster project, with no interim file saving or translating necessary.

Before You Scan: Configure PrintMaster for TWAIN Use

Before you use PrintMaster to manage your first scan, you have to configure the program for your specific scanner or digital camera. To do this, choose PrintMaster's File menu and click Select Source. When the Select Source dialog box appears, select the scanner or digital camera that you'll be using, and click OK.

To scan an image directly into a PrintMaster project, follow these steps:

1. Choose PrintMaster's File menu and select Acquire to start your scanner's built-in software.
2. Scan the picture according to the directions that came with your scanner.
3. If the Save Acquired Picture dialog box appears (and it won't always, depending on your scanner), enter a name and description for the scanned image, and then click OK.

Your scanned image now appears in your project, ready for placement or editing.

Scan It Small

When you're scanning images, try to keep your scanned files as small as possible. Large files not only use up valuable disk space; they also can slow down your screen display.

One way to reduce file size when scanning is to reduce the dots per inch (dpi) in your scanned image. The more dots per inch your scanner reads, the larger the file size (and the higher the resultant picture quality). Scanning at a dpi higher than what your printer can print is wasted detail. In fact, scans often look better if they're 50–100dpi less than your printer's maximum dpi.

Take a Digital Photo

Digital cameras differ from traditional cameras in that images are not saved to film; instead, images are saved digitally, on either floppy disks or special memory cards. These images can then be downloaded to your computer, and added to PrintMaster projects.

Although you can save your digital photos to standard files that can be imported into PrintMaster, you can also "acquire" photos automatically into a PrintMaster project, much as you can do with scanned images. To acquire a digital photograph directly into a PrintMaster project, follow these steps:

1. Choose PrintMaster's File menu and select Acquire to start your digital camera's built-in software.

2. Download the picture from your camera according to the directions that came with your digital camera.

3. If the Save Acquired Picture dialog box appears (and it won't always, depending on your camera software), enter a name and description for the digital photograph, and then click OK.

Your digital photograph now appears in your project, ready for placement or editing.

Managing Your Photographs with Photo Organizer

If you store a lot of photographs on your hard disk, it's easy to lose track of what is stored where. For that reason, PrintMaster 8.0 includes a new tool, *Photo Organizer*, that lets you organize your scanned and digital photos—and then find them quickly and easily when you need them for PrintMaster projects. In addition, Photo

Organizer lets you create electronic albums, produce slideshows, attach photos to your email, create simple Web pages, and more.

Upgrade to PrintMaster 8.0 for Photo Organizer

If you're looking for a single reason to upgrade from a previous version of PrintMaster to PrintMaster 8.0, Photo Organizer is it. If you work at all with photographs in your projects, you will find Photo Organizer invaluable for photo management, editing, and simple electronic output. It's a terrific tool!

When you click the Photo Organizer button in the File toolbar, Photo Organizer launches and presents you with its *Light Table*, as shown in Figure 8.3.

Get photographs from a hard disk file, CD-ROM, floppy disk, scanner, or digital camera.

Create new albums, emails, slideshows, Web pages, or printouts.

Send a picture to another graphics program.

FIG. 8.3

Use Photo Organizer to manage all your digital photographs.

Display the contents of the Light Table.

Search for a photograph.

Delete a file.

Album

Browser pane

Viewer pane

Presenter view

Gallery view

Catalog view

Details view

Export, resize, crop, rotate, refocus, color correct, and change the lighting of a picture.

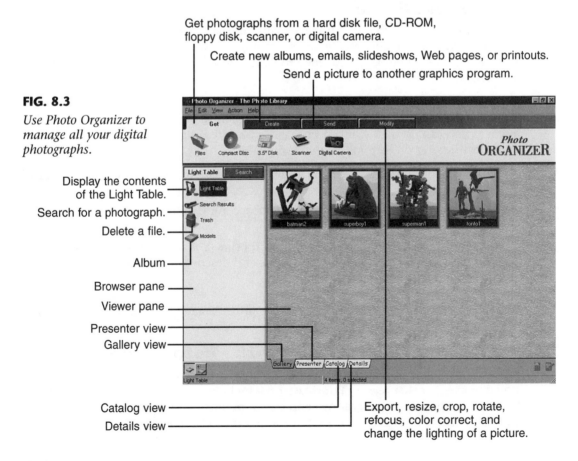

Changing Desktop Views

Photo Organizer's default desktop is called the Light Table. The Light Table is a workspace where you can organize and edit your pictures, and then store them in an *album.*

The contents of the Light Table or any open album are displayed in the Viewer pane. You can display the Viewer pane in a number of ways, all accessible from the View menu:

➤ **Gallery.** Displays thumbnails of your photographs.

➤ **Presenter.** Displays all the images in the selected slideshow.

➤ **Catalog.** Displays thumbnails of photographs *plus* file details.

➤ **Details.** Displays only file details (filename, location, size, and so on), no thumbnails.

Getting a Picture into the Program

You can transfer pictures from any media into Photo Organizer. When you add a picture to the program, it is placed on the Light Table; from there, it can be edited or placed in an album or slideshow.

To "get" a picture, click the Get tab, and then select the icon for the device that contains the picture. You can choose from files on your hard disk, files on a CD-ROM or Photo CD (Compact disc), files on a floppy disk (3.5-inch disk), scanned pictures (Scanner), or digital photographs from a digital camera. Photo Organizer lets you import pictures in the BMP, CLS, CMP, DCX, EPS, FPX, ICA, IMG, JPG, MAC, MSP, PCD, PCT, PCX, PNG, PSD, RAS, SFW, TGA, TIF, WMF, and WPG formats.

When you click a media icon, you're presented with the Import Photographs Wizard. Answer the questions in the wizard to find, label, and save the picture.

Editing a Picture

After a picture has been added to Photo Organizer, you have various editing options available to you. When you click the Modify tab, you can perform the following operations:

➤ **Save As.** Click this icon to display the Save As dialog box. From here, you can rename the selected image, save it in another file format, and save it to another album.

➤ **Resize.** Click this icon to display the Resize Images window, which lets you specify a new height and width for the selected image.

➤ **Crop.** Click this icon to display the Crop Image window. Cropping works differently in Photo Organizer than it does in the main PrintMaster program; simply click and drag your mouse to draw a box representing the final cropped area.

Click Save to save the newly cropped image (or Save As to save the cropped image in a different file).

➤ **Rotate.** Click this icon to display the Effects window with the Rotation option selected (see Figure 8.4.) Click a button to choose a preselected rotation angle, or enter a custom degree of rotation. Click Save or Save As when done. (This same window is used for other editing operations; click the Rotation button to select from Lighting, Focus, or Correction.)

FIG. 8.4

Rotating an image in the Effects window; this same window is used to edit lighting, focus, and other image correction.

➤ **Lighting.** Click this icon to display the Effects window with the Lighting option selected. Adjust the Brightness and Contrast sliders to your tastes, and then click the Save or Save As button.

➤ **Focus.** Click this icon to display the Effects window with the Focus option selected. Adjust the Focus slider to either Blur or Sharpen the image, and then click the Save or Save As button.

➤ **Correction.** Click this icon to display the Effects window with the Correction option selected. You can click a button to auto-correct the image's color or exposure, or use the sliders to manually adjust Red, Green, and Blue saturation. Click Save or Save As when finished.

Creating a New Album

Photo Organizer stores its images in *albums*. You can create multiple albums, each containing different types of pictures.

To create a new album, click the Create tab and select the Album icon. When the Create Album dialog box appears, enter a name for the album, select the appropriate options, and click OK.

Your new album appears in the Viewer pane, along with any previously created albums. To display the contents of an album on the Light Table, click the album's icon.

You can group multiple albums into *libraries*. To create a new library, choose the File menu and select New Library; to open an existing library, choose the File menu and select Open Library.

Printing a Picture

You can quickly and easily print any picture stored within Photo Organizer. Click the Send tab and select the Print icon. When the Print Images dialog box appears, select whether you want to create full-size prints or "index prints" that include multiple photographs on a single page. Click the Next button and follow the onscreen instructions to configure your printout and initiate printing.

Creating a Slideshow

You can use Photo Organizer to create continuously running Presenter™-format slideshows. When you create a slideshow, all necessary pictures and software can be transferred to a single floppy disk for distribution to family, friends, and business associates.

To create a slideshow, click the Create tab, and select the Slideshow icon. When the Publish Slideshow Wizard appears, follow the instructions to select the slideshow's pictures, destination, and viewer platform (Windows and/or Macintosh).

To view a slideshow, choose the View menu and select Slideshow. When the slideshow is displayed (see Figure 8.5), the slides automatically change every six seconds. You can manually change slides by clicking the appropriate Show Image buttons in the top-left corner of the slideshow; you can adjust the properties for your slideshow by clicking the Slideshow Options button and configuring the settings in the Slideshow Properties dialog box.

FIG. 8.5

Watching a Presenter slideshow.

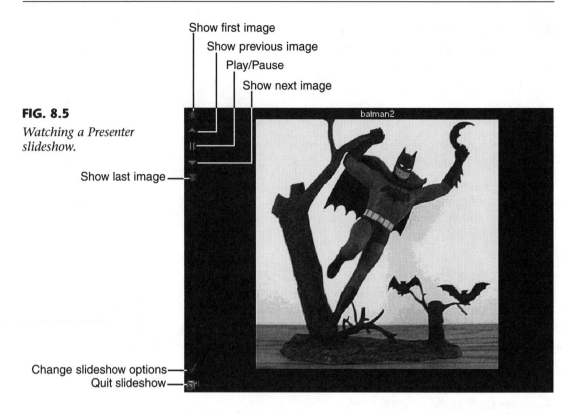

Show first image

Show previous image

Play/Pause

Show next image

Show last image

Change slideshow options

Quit slideshow

Sending a Picture via Email

You can use Photo Organizer to send a picture to anyone on the Internet via an attachment to an email message. Click the Create tab and select the Email icon to launch the Send Pictures via Electronic Mail Wizard. Follow the instructions in this wizard to identify your email service, dial-up Internet connection, mail server (SMTP server) name, sender name, sender email address, and pictures to send. When the Send Electronic Mail screen appears, enter the text of your message and your desired recipients, and then click the Send button. Photo Organizer now dials your Internet connection and sends the newly created email message—with your selected pictures attached.

Photographs with Regular Email

Although Photo Organizer creates a neat little photographic email postcard, you don't have to go to all the trouble of using Photo Organizer to send photographs over the Internet. Most email programs let you *attach* files of any type, including digital photographs, to email messages—and the process is typically easier and faster than creating a Photo Organizer email postcard.

Creating a Picture Web Page

Photo Organizer also lets you quickly create a series of Web pages to display selected pictures on the Internet. This is a surprisingly easy way to create a simple picture-oriented Web site.

Photo Organizer will create the following Web pages for you:

- ➤ **Home page.** The main page for your photo site, with links to all other pages you created.

- ➤ **Presentation pages.** Individual pages that display your photographs at full size. Each presentation page includes controls for viewing the next, previous, first, and last pictures in your collection.

- ➤ **Gallery page.** Displays thumbnail images of all photos on your site, complete with title, author's name, and date. As you can see in Figure 8.6, you can click a photo to view it on a full-size presentation page.

- ➤ **Summary page.** Similar to the Gallery page, except that it displays only a list of the photos, no thumbnails. Click a photo title to view the full-size presentation page.

- ➤ **Links page.** Lists links to any favorite sites you specify.

- ➤ **About page.** Displays your personal information, as well as an email link users can click to send you private messages.

To create Web pages with Photo Organizer, click the Create tab and select the Web Page icon. When the Publish Photos to Web Page Wizard appears, follow the onscreen instructions to create the pages you need.

FIG. 8.6

A Gallery page created with Photo Organizer.

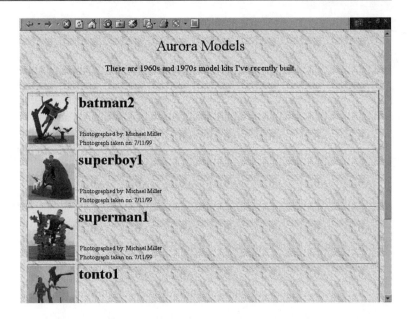

When using the wizard, you'll be asked to make the choices detailed in Table 8.2.

Table 8.2   Photo Organizer Web Page Options

Wizard Page	Action/Information Needed
Select Photographs	Select the photographs to include on your Web site.
Web Page Presentation Information	Enter titles for the Home and Gallery pages; a location to store the pages on your hard disk; and any additional text (comments) you want displayed on the Home page.
Information About You	Enter information for the About page, including your name, email address, and Web page address.
Web Pages to Create	Select which pages you want to create; the resolution you want to use to display your pictures; and any links to other pages for the Links page.
Page Appearance	Select text and background colors for your pages, as well as a background image (if desired).

Wizard Page	Action/Information Needed
Publish Web Pages	If you want Photo Organizer to upload your pages to a Web hosting service, enter information for the FTP server (host) and check the Automatically Upload My Pages to the Internet option; if you prefer to upload your pages manually, leave all options unchecked.

Photo Organizer now creates your Web pages and (if you selected the Automatically Upload option) uploads them to your Web page hosting service. (You can also upload the pages manually, using the services at your Web hosting site or a manual FTP program.) To view your pages, use your Web browser to either open the files on your hard disk (look in the C:\WEBPAGES\ folder) or on the Internet (after the pages have been uploaded).

Photo Workshop or PrintMaster: Which to Use to Create Web Pages

With PrintMaster 8.0 there are two ways to create Web pages—as a PrintMaster project, or as a Photo Organizer album. Which method should you use?

If you just need a simple Web site to display your photographs, use Photo Organizer. It doesn't give you many options in terms of design or layout—and if you want to edit the pages at a later time you have to use an HTML editing program—but it creates good-looking photo pages quickly and easily.

If you want a more sophisticated set of Web pages—or pages that are more than just a photo gallery—use the main PrintMaster program. You have a *lot* more choices in terms of layout and design, and the pages are easier to edit and update. You'll spend more time creating the pages, but you'll like the results!

To learn how to create Web pages with PrintMaster, see Chapter 16, "Create and Publish Personal Web Pages."

Editing Your Photographs with Photo Workshop

If you think Photo Organizer has some neat picture-management features, you'll be even more impressed by the advanced picture-editing features in another new PrintMaster 8.0 tool, *Photo Workshop*. This easy-to-use tool lets you manipulate and edit your photos and other bitmap images to eliminate red eye, increase sharpness, adjust brightness, and change colors and textures.

Photo Workshop Edits More Than Just Photos

Photo Workshop can edit any image in BMP, EPS, JPG, TIF, or WMF format.

To launch Photo Workshop, select the picture to edit and then click the Photo Workshop button in the Edit toolbar. When the pop-up menu appears, select the kind of editing you want to perform.

Photo Workshop now launches with that particular editing tool selected. After Photo Workshop is running, you can change to any editing tool by selecting the appropriate tab.

Crop, Shape, and Rotate

When you select the Crop/Orientation tab shown in Figure 8.7, you have access to the following operations:

FIG. 8.7

Cropping and rotating a photograph.

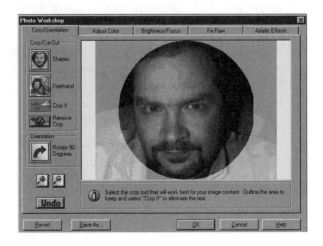

➤ **Crop to a shape.** Click the Shapes button to display the pop-up palette, and then click the shape you want to use to frame your image. The shape you selected is now superimposed on your image; use the cursor to resize or reposition the crop area. Click the Crop It button to preview the cropped picture and—if you like what you see—click OK to place the cropped picture back in your project or Save As to save it as a new file. If you want to undo the crop, click the Remove Crop button.

➤ **Freehand crop.** Click the Freehand button and use the cursor to draw a series of lines around the area you want cropped; double-click to automatically finish the shape with a final line back to the starting point. If necessary, drag the handles on your shape to edit the crop area. Click the Crop It button to preview the cropped picture and—if you like what you see—click OK to place the cropped picture back in your project or Save As to save it as a new file. If you want to undo the crop, click the Remove Crop button.

➤ **Rotate your picture.** Click the Rotate 90 Degrees button to turn your picture 90 degrees counterclockwise.

Recolor and Uncolor

When you select the Adjust Color tab, shown in Figure 8.8, you have access to the following operations:

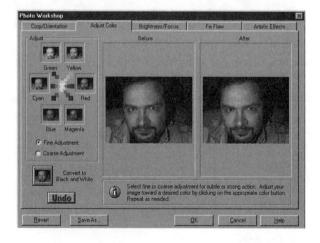

FIG. 8.8

Recoloring a photograph— or removing all color completely.

➤ **Adjust the color.** You can increase (individually) the red, yellow, green, cyan, blue, or magenta in a picture by clicking the appropriate button in the Adjust section. (To make small changes, make sure Fine Adjustment is checked; to make big changes, check Coarse Adjustment.) Your changes are reflected in the After pane. Click OK to place the recolored picture back in your project, or click Save As to save it as a new file.

➤ **Create a black-and-white picture.** To remove all color from the picture—a good idea if you're going to be printing on a black-and-white printer—click the Convert to Black and White button. Click OK to place the monochrome picture back in your project, or click Save As to save it as a new file.

Adjust Brightness, Contrast, and Sharpness

When you select the Brightness/Focus tab, shown in Figure 8.9, you have access to the following operations:

FIG. 8.9

Adjusting the brightness, contrast, and sharpness of a picture.

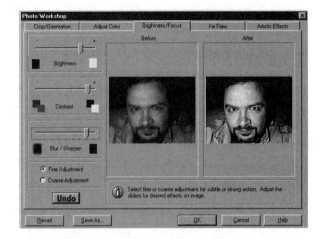

➤ **Adjust picture brightness.** Move the Brightness slider to the left to make the picture darker; move it to the right to make the picture lighter.

➤ **Adjust picture contrast.** Move the Contrast slider to the left to decrease the picture's contrast; move it to the right to increase the contrast.

Brightness and Contrast Work Together

If you adjust a picture's brightness, you'll probably want to adjust the contrast, as well. These two adjustments work hand in hand, and changing one often affects the other.

➤ **Blur or sharpen the picture.** Move the Blur/Sharpen slider to the left to make the picture less sharp; move it to the right to make the picture more sharp.

Click OK to place the readjusted picture back in your project, or click Save As to save it as a new file.

Fix Common Picture Flaws

When you select the Fix Flaw tab, shown in Figure 8.10, you have access to the following operations:

FIG. 8.10

Fixing red eye, pet eye, scratches, and shiny faces.

➤ **Remove red eye.** To remove red eye (caused by flash photography), click the Red Eye button; when the pop-up menu appears, click the point that best matches the size of the eyes in your photograph, and then click the center of an eye in your photo.

➤ **Remove pet eye.** To remove pet eye (red eye in photos of animals), click the Pet Eye button; when the pop-up menu appears, click the point that best matches the size of the eyes in your photograph, and then click the center of an eye in your photo.

➤ **Remove dust and scratches.** Click the Dust and Scratch button; when the pop-up menu appears, select a pointer size. Move your cursor over the area of the photo containing dust or scratch marks, and then click your mouse button.

➤ **Correct shiny faces.** To remove shininess caused by flash photography, click the Shiny Face button; when the pop-up menu appears, select the pointer that best matches the size of the shiny area. Move your cursor over the shiny area, and then click your mouse button.

Click OK to place the readjusted picture back in your project, or click Save As to save it as a new file.

Apply Artistic Effects

When you select the Artistic Effects tab, shown in Figure 8.11, you can apply a variety of special effects to your photograph, including the following:

FIG. 8.11

Just some of the special effects available on Photo Workshop's Artistic Effects tab.

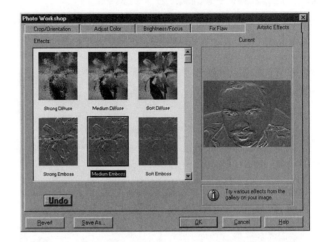

➤ Antique

➤ Contrast

➤ Diffuse

➤ Emboss

➤ Noise

➤ Pixelate

➤ Stitch

All effects can be applied in soft, medium, or strong versions.

To apply an effect, just select the effect, and then preview how it looks. If you want to keep the effect, click OK to place the readjusted picture back in your project, or click Save As to save it as a new file. If you want to undo the effect, click the Undo button.

Don't Overdo the Effects

Photo Workshop's special effects are neat, but easily overused. Effects should be used for *effect*, not as a regular thing, or they lose their impact. In addition, too strong an effect can obscure your original picture, which probably isn't your intent. In other words—don't get *too* artistic with your effects!

In the Next Chapter...

Now that you know how to work with photographs and other types of pictures, let's learn how to work with text. See Chapter 9, "Better Text," for more.

Better Text

Virtually every project you create will include some text—even if it's just a headline. Some projects—such as newsletters—will include a lot of text. To maximize the visual appeal of your projects, you need to know not only how to add text, but also how to format it for maximum impact.

Working with Text Boxes

You add text to a PrintMaster project by using a *text box,* a rectangular element that contains nothing but text. You can edit and format the text within a text box, and you can format the background and border of the text box itself.

All text—within a single text box—functions together as a unit, and you can add any number of text boxes to your projects. Figure 9.1 shows a typical text box within a PrintMaster project.

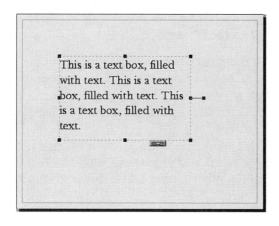

FIG. 9.1

A text box is just another element—grab the selection handles to resize the box, or use the rotation handle to rotate the text.

Create a New Text Box

To add a new text box to a project, click the Text Box button on the Edit toolbar or choose the Add button and select Text Box. Use your cursor to draw the text box on your page.

After the text box is drawn, a blinking "edit" cursor appears within the box. To enter text in the text box, position your cursor at the edit point and begin typing.

If you want to edit the text in a preexisting text box, select the element, position your cursor where you want to start editing, and then double-click. The edit cursor now appears, and you can edit, add, or delete text in this particular text box.

You can also import text from another program directly into a text box. Just position your cursor at the insert point in a predrawn text box, choose the Edit menu, and click Import Text. When the Open dialog box appears, select the file to import, and then click Open. If you're importing a lot of text, you may need to resize the text box to fit, or continue the text in another text box (discussed later in this chapter).

Import TXT or RTF Files Only

PrintMaster allows you to import only TXT or RTF files, so you may have to export the text from your word processor into one of these file formats if you want to import that text into PrintMaster.

Connect Multiple Text Boxes

If you have a long block of text, you may want to flow the text into a second (or even third!) text box elsewhere on your page. You do this by *connecting* the text boxes.

Flow Your Text

Flowing text from one part of the page to another part—or from one page to another page—is a good way to handle long blocks of text in a brochure, newsletter, or Web page.

To connect two text boxes, click the Link icon at the bottom of the first text box; your cursor becomes a *Text Flow* icon (with an "X" over it). Move the Text Flow icon over the second text box (you can link only to *empty* text boxes) and click your mouse button. Any excess text from the first text box now flows into the second text box.

To disconnect a text box, select both that text box (first) and then the previous text box it is connected to. Click the Link button on the main text box and the flowed text disappears from the (now) previously connected text box.

Format a Text Box

In addition to formatting the text itself, you can also format the text box that contains the text, just as you would any other PrintMaster element. Just select the text box (*not* the text inside!) and then use the Fill Color, Line Format, and Shadow Format buttons as appropriate.

There are also some formatting commands specific to text boxes. With the text box selected, choose the Format menu and select Text Box. When the Text Box Formatting dialog box appears, you can make the following adjustments:

➤ **Margins.** To set the top, bottom, left, and right margins *within* the text box, enter values (in inches) in the appropriate entry boxes.

➤ **Columns.** To format your text in multiple columns, enter the Number of columns, as well as the Spacing *between* columns (in inches). (When you use columns, your text fills up the first column first, and then flows to the second column—the columns themselves are not automatically balanced.)

➤ **Vertical alignment.** If you want the text to align at the top of the text box, choose the Vertical Alignment list and select Top Aligned; you can also select to have your text Middle Aligned (centered) or Bottom Aligned.

➤ **Shape.** You're not limited to a rectangular text box; you can select from a number of interesting shapes that the text within the text box will follow. Just select a shape from the Shape list; see Figure 9.2 for an example. (You can also adjust the text shape directly by choosing the Format menu and selecting Text Shape.)

Click OK to apply your formatting.

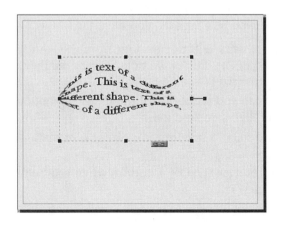

FIG. 9.2

A text box of a different shape is shown here.

111

Wrap Text Around Other Elements

If you layer another element on top of a text box, you can format the text in the text box to wrap around the graphic in a number of different ways. (Of course, you can also have the uppermost graphic just obscure the text below—but this is seldom a desired approach.)

Actually, text wrapping is applied to the elements that sit above the text box, not to the text box itself. After you set text wrapping for an element, all text boxes on lower layers wrap around the element.

To turn on text wrapping, make sure the text is on a lower layer and the graphic element is on the *top* layer of your project, and then select the graphic element (*not* the text box!). Choose the Arrange menu and select Text Wrap. When the Text Wrap dialog box appears, select either Text Wraps to Bounds or Text Wraps to Shape (these both have the same effect). If you select Text Flows Over, you're effectively turning *off* text wrapping.

Top Align to Wrap

For text to wrap around an element, the text must be aligned at the top of its text box. Make sure you set the text box's vertical alignment to Top Aligned.

Formatting Your Text

You can format the text *within* a text box in a number of ways. Make sure you select the *text* you want to format with your cursor, and *not* the text box itself!

Format Fonts

To change the type, style, size, color, or effect of your font, choose the Format menu and select Font. When the Font dialog box appears, you have the following options:

➤ **Font type.** Select the Font tab and select a new font from the Font list. The font you choose is previewed in the Preview section. (Check the Preview Actual Size option to preview at actual size.)

➤ **Font style.** Select the Font tab and select one of the following options from the Font Style list: Regular, Bold, Italic, or Bold Italic.

➤ **Size.** Select the Font tab and select a size from the Size list, or manually enter a specific size in the Size box.

➤ **Color.** Select the Font tab and click the Color button; when the Color Palette dialog box appears, select a new color.

➤ **Fill pattern.** Select the Effects tab and select a new pattern from the Fill Pattern list to add a pattern to your text. (This option should be applied only to larger font sizes.) Click the Color button to select a color for the pattern.

➤ **Underline.** Select the Font tab and check the Underline option to underline the selected text.

➤ **White border.** Select the Font tab and check the White Border option to put a simple white border around your text; this is a good option when you have dark text against a dark background.

➤ **Text outline.** Select the Effects tab and select an outline type from the Outline list. Click the Color button to select a color for the border.

➤ **Shadow.** Select the Effects tab and select a shadow type from the Shadow list. Click the Color button to select a color for the shadow.

A Font of Knowledge

A font is, technically, a specific combination of typeface and style. Each typeface has a name (such as Helvetica or Times Roman), and can be printed in specific styles (such as bold or italic). Different fonts have different impacts in your printed documents; you generally want to use serif fonts (fonts that have those little decorations on the ends of letters, such as Times New Roman) for body text, and sans serif fonts (fonts without those little decorations, such as Arial) for headlines. You also don't want to use too many fonts in a single project; it makes the page harder to read, plus it takes more time to print!

Space Characters

To change the spacing between characters, select the text to format, choose the Format menu, and select Character Spacing. When the Character Spacing dialog box appears, select an option to make your text looser or tighter—or select a custom spacing percentage.

Stretch Text

You can stretch text to fill the width of a text box. This changes both the size and shape of the selected characters; letters increase in height as they stretch in width. Just select the text and click the Stretch button on the Edit toolbar—or choose the Format menu, and check Stretching. (To unstretch text, uncheck Stretching.)

Set Tabs

To set tab stops in your text, choose the Format menu and select Tabs. When the Tabs dialog box appears, enter the position of the tab stop (in inches from the left margin) in the Position box. Select the Alignment of the tab (left, center, right, or aligned to a decimal point) and choose whether the tab should have a leader character. Then, click the Set button. Repeat this procedure to set multiple tab stops for the selected text. To delete a stop, select a tab in the Tab Stops list and click the Clear button.

Add Bullets and Numbering

To display selected text as a bulleted list, choose the Format menu and select Bullets & Numbering. When the Bullets and Numbering dialog box appears, select the Bullets tab, select a bullet style, and then click the OK button. (You can also select the Custom Bullet button to choose from a larger selection of bullets.)

To display selected text as a numbered list, choose the Format menu and select Bullets & Numbering. When the Bullets and Numbering dialog box appears, select the Numbers tab, select a number style, and then click the OK button.

As you add new paragraphs to the selected text, the new paragraphs continue with the bullet or number style you selected.

Add a Drop Cap

To add a drop cap to the beginning of a paragraph, position your cursor anywhere in the paragraph, choose the Format menu, select Drop Caps, and then select how many lines you want the drop cap to drop. Remove a drop cap by selecting None as the drop.

Add Symbols

In addition to straight text, you can also add various symbols (such as bullets, arrows, and check marks) to a text box. To add a symbol, choose the Format menu and select Insert Symbol. When the Insert Symbol dialog box appears, select the character you want to add to your project, and then click OK.

Add Today's Date

To automatically insert today's date into your text, choose the Format menu and select Insert Date. PrintMaster automatically places today's date in your text, in the format mm/dd/yy.

Format Paragraphs

PrintMaster lets you format entire paragraphs, in addition to chunks of text. Select the paragraph(s) to format, choose the Format menu, and then select Paragraph. When the Paragraph Formatting dialog box appears, you can change the following settings:

➤ **Indentation.** This setting allows you to specify a minimum distance (in inches) between the text and the left and right sides of the text box. You can also set the indentation for the first line of the selected paragraph(s); set a negative value to create a *hanging indent*.

➤ **Alignment.** Pull down this list and select from Left Aligned, Centered, Right Aligned, or Justified text.

➤ **Line Spacing.** This setting determines the spacing between lines, in either lines or points. For example, to double-space your text, select 2 lines as the line spacing value.

➤ **Paragraph Spacing.** This setting allows you to control the space before and after selected paragraphs, in inches.

Add Powerful Headlines

Although you could format the text in a text box to serve as the headline for a project, PrintMaster has a special Headline tool that offers more sophisticated headline effects. You activate this tool by clicking the Headline button on the Edit toolbar, or by choosing the Add menu and selecting Headline.

When the Create a Headline dialog box appears (see Figure 9.3), enter the text for your headline in the Enter Headline Text Here box. If you want to select from PrintMaster's preselected headline styles, click the ReadyMade option button and then select from one of the displayed styles. If you want to create your own headline style, click the Customize option button and use the Face, Shape, Position, Outline, Depth, and Proportion tabs to fine-tune the details of your headline. Monitor the preview of your headline, and click OK to add the headline to your project. After you add the headline, it can be repositioned, resized, or rotated just as you would any other element.

115

FIG. 9.3

Creating a fancy headline with the Create a Headline dialog box is easy.

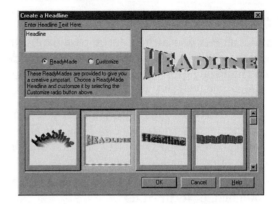

Extra Long Headlines Are Quite Often Very Hard to Read and Have Little Impact on the Reader, Some Say

Get the point? For maximum impact, keep your headlines short!

Display Information in Tables

A table is a grid with columns, rows, and cells that you use to display text and numbers in an organized format. Figure 9.4 shows a typical table with four rows and three columns. To add a table to your project, follow these steps:

FIG. 9.4

This three-column, four-row table is formatted in Checkbook Register style.

Cell 1	Cell 2	Cell 3
113.2	270.5	315.7
432.7	467.2	485.2
100.2	150.5	160.4

1. Click the Table button in the Edit toolbar, or choose the Add button and select Table.

2. Use your cursor to draw the outline of the table in your project; when you release the mouse button, the Create Table dialog box appears.

3. Select the number of rows and columns you want in your table.

4. Select a format for your table.

5. Click OK to create the table to your specifications.

6. Position your cursor in a table cell to enter text or numbers in the cell. Use the Tab key to move from cell to cell.

After the table is created, you can resize the rows and columns. Just position your cursor over a borderline until it changes shape, and then drag the row or column border to the new position. To insert a new row or column next to an existing one, select the entire row or column, choose the Table menu, select Insert, and make the appropriate choices in the Insert dialog box. To delete a row or column, select the row or column to delete, choose the Table menu, and then select Delete Row or Delete Column.

To change the format of the entire table, select the table, choose the Table menu, select AutoFormat, and select a new format from the Auto Format dialog box. To format a single cell (or group of cells), select the cell(s), choose the Table menu, select Cell Formatting, and then select new fill and line options in the Cell Formatting dialog box.

Use Tables for Numbers

If you're displaying a lot of numbers—such as a profit and loss statement for a business—you *could* just use a normal text box with tabs, but you'll find it both easier and better-looking to use a table to organize and align the multiple rows and columns of numbers.

Check Your Spelling

It doesn't hurt to check the spelling of the text in your project; there's nothing more embarrassing than sending out a batch of brochures or invitations containing blatant misspellings!

You can check the spelling in your entire document by clicking the Check Spelling button in the File toolbar or by choosing the Tools menu and selecting Check Spelling. If the spell checker comes across a word it doesn't recognize, it highlights the word and displays the Check Spelling dialog box. At this point, you have the

117

option to Ignore the possible misspelling; Ignore All instances of this particular possible misspelling; Change the word to one from the Suggestions list or to whatever you enter in the Change To box; Change All instances of this misspelling; Add the highlighted word to PrintMaster's spelling dictionary; or Close the dialog box and halt the spell check.

In the Next Chapter...

Beyond lines, pictures, and text, PrintMaster includes several other tools you can use to add spice to your projects. Turn to Chapter 10, "Better Projects with PrintMaster's Special Tools," to learn more.

Better Projects with PrintMaster's Special Tools

In addition to everything you can do within the PrintMaster program itself—creating and editing projects and project elements—PrintMaster also includes some "add in" tools that provide even more functionality for your projects. Read on to learn more about these useful tools.

Manage Your Contacts with the Address Book

PrintMaster's Address Book is a tool attached to a small database that lets you store your most important contacts, and then use that contact information to create merged mailings for special PrintMaster projects. For example, you can insert names from your Address Book into personalized Christmas cards or invitations.

You open the Address Book by clicking the Address Book button in the Hub.

Adding Names to the Address Book

When the Address Book window appears, click the New Entry button. This displays a blank contact form, as shown in Figure 10.1. From here, just position your cursor over the first *field* (First Name) and start entering information. Press the Tab key to move from field to field; there are lots of fields, so you'll have to scroll down to see them all. When the form is completed, click the New Entry button again to register the information you just entered and open a new form for your next contact.

FIG. 10.1

Use the Address Book to store personal information for family and friends.

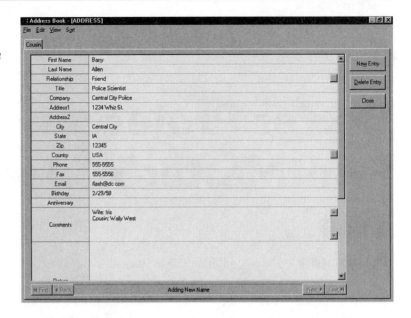

The following fields are available in the Address Book (although you don't have to fill them all in if you don't want to):

➤ First Name

➤ Last Name

➤ Relationship (Click the button in this field to select from four predefined relationships: Client, Family, Friend, and Vendor.)

➤ Title

➤ Company

➤ Address1 (Use for the main street address.)

➤ Address2 (Use for long addresses, or apartment numbers.)

➤ City

➤ State

➤ Zip

➤ Country (Click the button in this field to select from a list of countries.)

➤ Phone

➤ Fax

➤ Email

➤ Birthday

➤ Anniversary

➤ Comments (Enter anything here you want.)

120

➤ Picture (Click the New button to select a photo to add; click the Clear button to delete an existing picture; click the Copy button to copy the picture for use in another application.)

➤ User Defined Info (Enter any information you want.)

➤ User Defined Date (Enter any date you want.)

You can navigate from contact to contact by using the Next and Back arrow buttons; use the First and Last arrow buttons to go to the very first and last contacts in your Address Book.

To delete an entry, go to that entry and click the Delete Entry button. Click the Close button to close the Address Book.

Importing Names from Other Programs

If you already have a list of contacts in another program, you can import them into the PrintMaster Address Book—eliminating the need to retype all that information. You can import text files in which the information is stored in either comma- or tab-delimited formats (which means you first have to *export* the contact data from your other program into a comma- or tab-delimited text file).

To import a contact file, choose the Address Book's File menu and select Import. This opens the Import Names Wizard; follow the wizard's onscreen instructions to successfully import a list of names.

You can also save your PrintMaster Address Book in a text file, which can then be imported into other programs. Just choose the File menu and select Save As; when the Save As dialog box appears, choose the Save As Type list and select *.txt to save as a tab-delimited text file or *.csv to save as a comma-delimited text file.

Viewing and Sorting Your Contacts

You can view your Address Book contacts in one of two ways:

➤ **One at a Time.** The standard view for text entry.

➤ **Overview.** Lists all your contacts in a table or spreadsheet-like format.

To change the Address Book view, choose the View menu and select the view you want.

By default, PrintMaster automatically organizes your Address Book entries by relationship, with a separate tab for each type of relationship. You can sort your Address Book by any field, however; tabs appear for whichever field you choose to sort on. To change your sort field, choose the Sort menu and select a field. Click a tab to see all entries that match that particular sort field.

Merging Information

You can merge information from any field in your Address Book into any PrintMaster project. All you have to do is add a *Fill-In Field* or *Mail Merge Field* to your project. This is a great way to create a personalized holiday card or add contact information to labels or envelopes. Just follow these steps:

1. From your project's Design Workspace, click the Text Box button (or choose the Add menu and select Text Box) and draw a text box in your project.

2. With the new text box selected, choose the Tools menu, select Fill-In Fields, and then select Add Fill-In Field.

3. When the Add Field or Merge Field dialog box appears, select the field name you want to add and click the Insert button. This places the name of the field within your text box. You can insert multiple fields into your text box; click OK when you are done.

When you're ready to print your project, click the Print button and click the Merge Names button in the Print dialog box. Select the names from your Address Book that you want to print, or click the Select All button to select every name in your Address Book. Click the OK button, and then click the Print button in the Print dialog box. PrintMaster prints multiple copies of your project, each copy personalized with the information you selected.

Prompt Yourself with the Event Reminder

The information in your Address Book also serves another function; PrintMaster automatically monitors the dates entered in your Address Book and notifies you of any important events coming up—birthdays, anniversaries, and so on. The Event Reminder monitors all dates entered in your Address Book.

In addition, the Event Reminder lets you set up freestanding events to be monitored. All you have to do is choose PrintMaster's Tools menu and select Event Reminder. When the Events dialog box appears, click the Event Reminder List button. To add a new event, click the New button and follow the instructions in the Event Reminder Wizard. To change an event, select the event in the Events dialog box and click the Change button. To delete an event, select it and click the Delete button.

Add Historical Information from the Year You Were Born

If you need ready-made information to add to a newsletter or birthday card or other project, you can use the Year You Were Born tool to automatically add historical information to your project. This tool can add the following information:

➤ Birthstone for a specific birthday

➤ Chinese Year—such as "Year of the...", and what that means for those born that year

➤ Entertainment highlights for the specified year—Nobel Prize winner, best-selling fiction book, best-selling nonfiction book, Best Picture, Best Director, Best Actress, and Best Actor Oscars

➤ Famous People—celebrities born on the same date

➤ Introduction—a brief lead-in for your project ("A Look at the World When So-and-So Was Born")

➤ News—top headlines for the specified year

➤ Sports—that year's champions in baseball, football, basketball, hockey, golf, tennis, and more

➤ Zodiac—the star sign (and accompanying information) for that specific date

Follow these steps to add Year You Were Born information to a project:

1. From within your projects Design Workspace, click the Year You Were Born button (or choose the Tools menu and select The Year You Were Born).

2. When The Year You Were Born dialog box appears, enter the person's name and birthday, select which items you want to include, and click OK.

3. The information you selected is now added to your project, in a pleasing layout, such as the one shown in Figure 10.2.

FIG. 10.2

Create automatic information with the Year You Were Born tool.

Try to pick only as much information as will easily fit within your project. For example, don't add *all* available information to a small greeting card!

Insert Prewritten Greetings with the Sentiment Gallery

When you're at a loss for words, let PrintMaster supply the words for you! PrintMaster's Sentiment Gallery contains thousands of preselected greetings you can add to greeting cards and other similar projects. Each *sentiment* contains two separate but related phrases—one appears on the front of the project and the other appears on the inside.

To add a sentiment to your project, follow these steps:

1. From your project's Design Workspace, click the Sentiment button on the Format toolbar (or choose the Add button and select Sentiment).

2. When the Sentiment Gallery appears (see Figure 10.3), select the Collection, Category, and Tone you desire—or search for a sentiment by Keyword. Use the scrollbar to scroll through all the matching sentiments.

FIG. 10.3

Select front and back sentiments to add to your project.

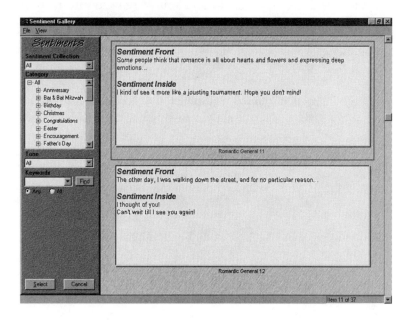

3. When you find the sentiment you want, highlight it and then click the Select button.

After the sentiment has been added to your project, you can format it as you would any element in your project.

Make Funny Faces with Cartoon-O-Matic

Sentiments are fine, but sometimes a picture is worth a thousand words. Fortunately, PrintMaster includes a tool that lets you create your own cartoon faces, which can add much-needed humor to your project!

To use the Cartoon-O-Matic tool, follow these steps:

1. From your project's Design Workspace, click the Cartoon-O-Matic button (or choose the Add button and select Cartoon-O-Matic Picture).

2. When the Cartoon-O-Matic window appears (as shown in Figure 10.4), click the New button. When the preview window appears, use the left and right arrows to cycle through the cartoon faces; click the New button to choose a new face.

Preview window

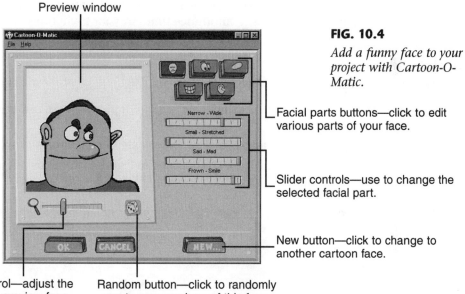

FIG. 10.4

Add a funny face to your project with Cartoon-O-Matic.

Facial parts buttons—click to edit various parts of your face.

Slider controls—use to change the selected facial part.

New button—click to change to another cartoon face.

Zoom control—adjust the size of the preview face.

Random button—click to randomly create new versions of this face.

3. Click one of the facial parts buttons to select a part of the face to change. (Different faces have different facial parts.)

4. Use the slider controls to change the various attributes of the selected facial part. (Different facial parts have different attributes to adjust.)

5. When you're finished creating your face, click the OK button to add the cartoon to your project.

To edit a completed face, just double-click it in the Design Workspace.

More Faces Available

You can download additional faces for Cartoon-O-Matic from the Web site of nFX (www.nfx.com), the company that created Cartoon-O-Matic.

Add Seals and Timepieces with Custom Graphics

PrintMaster 8.0 adds a new feature called *Custom Graphics*, which lets you add seals and timepieces to your projects. Use the seals to make certificates and other projects look more official; use the clocks to announce times in your invitations and such.

Add a Seal

To add a seal to your project, follow these steps:

1. From the Design Workspace, click the Custom Graphics button (on the Edit toolbar).
2. When the pop-up menu appears, click Seal.
3. When the Create a Seal dialog box appears (see Figure 10.5), enter the text for the top and bottom of your seal.

FIG. 10.5

Create official-looking seals for your projects.

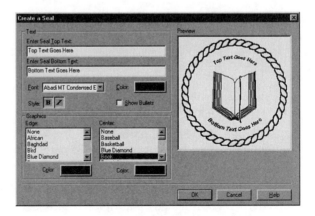

4. Choose a font, color, and style (bold or italic) for your seal text.
5. If you want to display decorative marks between your top and bottom text, check the Show Bullets check box.

126

6. Select which (if any) graphics you want to display around the edge or in the center of your seal; change the color of the graphics, if desired.

7. Click OK to add the completed seal to your project.

To modify a completed seal, double-click it—and then change any or all settings in the Create a Seal dialog box.

Add a Timepiece

To add a timepiece or clock to your project, follow these steps:

1. From the Design Workspace, click the Custom Graphics button (on the Edit toolbar).

2. When the pop-up menu appears, click Timepiece.

3. When the Create a Timepiece dialog box appears (see Figure 10.6), select the type of clock you want to display.

FIG. 10.6

Announce a starting time with a PrintMaster time-piece.

4. Set the time for your clock.

5. Click OK to add the clock to your project.

To modify a completed timepiece, just double-click it and make the appropriate changes in the Create a Timepiece dialog box.

In the Next Chapter...

In this section, you've learned how to add and edit all the different types of PrintMaster elements—including those elements created with PrintMaster's special tools. Now, it's time to start creating specific types of projects. Let's start with some projects your children will enjoy, presented in Chapter 11, "Projects for Kids."

PrintMaster

PART 3

Get Creative: How to Create Different Types of Projects

Projects for Kids

PrintMaster's projects can help your children turn a rainy afternoon into something fun and creative! From bookmarks, mobiles, and other crafts to book report covers, dioramas, and other homework helpers, PrintMaster offers hundreds of projects for children of all ages.

Fun for Kids

Most of PrintMaster's ready-made child-oriented projects are grouped into the Fun for Kids project type. To open a Fun for Kids project, go to the Hub and select Ready-Made. When the Project Gallery appears, choose the Project Type list and select Fun for Kids. Within Fun for Kids, you can choose from among the following categories of projects:

➤ Bookmarks
➤ Letterhead
➤ Masks
➤ Mobiles
➤ Puppets
➤ Stickers

These ready-made projects are ideal for smaller children, because most don't need any modification and can be printed as is.

Bookmarks

PrintMaster includes 24 different ready-made bookmarks, like the one shown in Figure 11.1. You'll want to print the bookmarks on a sturdy card stock for durability—or even laminate them!

FIG. 11.1

One of PrintMaster's 24 ready-made bookmarks—printing three to a page.

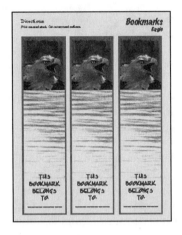

Each bookmark comes three to a page; you'll need to cut the three bookmarks out of the background sheet with a pair of scissors. The bookmarks are single-sided, so if you want a double-sided bookmark you might want to tape two bookmarks together, back-to-back.

To create your own bookmark design, the easiest way is to start with one of the simpler ready-made bookmarks. I recommend that you open the Boy Bookmark project, because it's relatively easy to edit to your liking. You'll want to ungroup all the graphics on the page, so select all three of the bookmarks, choose the Arrange menu, and select Ungroup. After the graphics are ungrouped, delete the "boy" artwork on each of the bookmarks. You can now edit the bookmarks to change backgrounds and borders, or add other graphics. Remember to add graphics to all three bookmarks separately; you can make this task easy by copying graphics from one bookmark and pasting them onto the others. Save your project when you're done, and then print out your new bookmarks!

Chessboard

PrintMaster includes a special Chessboard project, which is a red-and-black checkered background you can use for checkers or chess. The Chessboard project is found in the Project Gallery in the Puppets category.

You should print the Chessboard at 130% Output Size, and on heavy card stock. After you cut the Chessboard out of the background, paste it onto a heavy piece of cardboard. You may also want to laminate this project, or use clear wrapping tape to shield the surface against heavy use.

Letterhead

Children love to write notes on their own personal letterhead. PrintMaster includes 17 different premade letterhead designs, such as the one shown in Figure 11.2. Some of these are full letter-size letterheads; some are memo-sized, printing two pieces of stationery on a single sidewise 8 1/2-×11-inch sheet of paper. (If you use one of these half-sized letterheads, you'll have to cut the pieces of paper in half for use.)

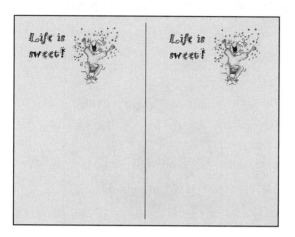

FIG. 11.2

Use PrintMaster's ready-made letterhead to create your own personal notes—this particular design prints two half-sized pieces on a single sheet.

If you want to create your own letterhead from scratch, go to the Hub and click the Brand New button. When the New Project dialog box appears, select Letterhead and click Next. When the Orientation dialog box appears, select Tall and click Finish. You now see a blank sheet of paper in the Design Workspace. Click the Art Gallery button in the Format toolbar to add graphics; see Chapter 6, "Better Backgrounds," to learn how to add a background color to your letterhead.

Don't Make Your Letterhead *Too* Fancy...

Remember that the main thing you do with letterhead is write on it—so if you fill up the entire page with fancy artwork, you won't leave enough room for your messages! Try to keep your artwork at the top or bottom or as a border along the sides; resist the urge to put a background graphic in the middle of your writing space. Along the same lines, if you want to print a color background on your stationery, pick a light color, because it's hard to read writing against a dark background.

Masks

PrintMaster includes 24 fun masks you can print and then cut out to use, such as the Frog mask shown in Figure 11.3. Print your masks on a heavy card stock for durability, cut the masks out of the background, cut out the indicated eye holes, and then punch small holes in the masks for the string that holds the mask in place. Remember to make the eye holes big enough to see out of; if the mask is for a smaller child, you may need to enlarge or reposition the eye holes for safety.

FIG. 11.3

The Frog mask—make sure you cut out the eye holes before you put it on!

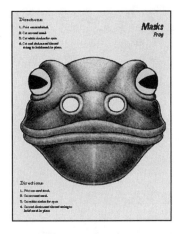

You can also create a mask from scratch, using PrintMaster's Cartoon-O-Matic tool. Start with a Brand New project, select Blank Page from the New Project dialog box, and select Tall from the Orientation dialog box. After the blank page appears in the Design Workspace, click the Cartoon-O-Matic button on the Format toolbar. Use Cartoon-O-Matic (discussed in Chapter 10, "Better Projects with PrintMaster's Special Tools") to create a face for your mask, and then click OK to add the face to your blank page. Resize the face to occupy the entire page, and then save and print your project. You can cut out the Cartoon-O-Matic face as you would a ready-made mask; you'll have to locate and size the eye holes and string holes yourself, however.

Who Was That Masked Man?

To create a traditional "Lone Ranger"–type mask, go to the Hub and select Brand New. When the New Project dialog box appears, select Craft and click Next. When the Choose a Craft Type dialog box appears, select Mask and click Finish. Color the mask as appropriate, then print, cut, and string it to create the perfect disguise!

Mobiles

PrintMaster includes seven different mobiles you can print and hang in your children's room. Each mobile—such as the one shown in Figure 11.4—contains a large top element and a half-dozen or more small hanging elements, and prints on multiple pages. You should print a mobile on heavy cardboard stock, and use string to hang the lower elements from the upper elements.

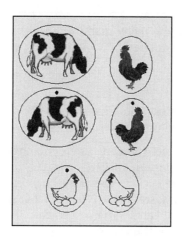

FIG. 11.4

Some of the pieces of a PrintMaster mobile—print, cut, and hang!

Back-to-Back Pieces

Mobiles have two sides, but are *not* double-sided projects. That means you print out all the parts of the mobile, and then glue the matching pieces back-to-back.

If you want to create your own mobile design, start with any of the ready-made mobiles (I like the nice elliptical shapes in the Butterfly Garden) and delete all the graphics from all the mobile elements. This leaves you with blank elliptical elements, on which you can place your own graphics.

Puppets and Figures

PrintMaster includes two ready-made finger puppet projects (Dinosaurs and Holiday Figures) in the Fun for Kids category, which can also be used as stand-up figures. Print these projects on heavy paper stock, for better durability. After you print out the puppets (which come eight to a page), cut the puppets out of the background, and then bend the puppets around your finger and tape the sides together. (If you're using these as stand-up figures, use heavy stock and bend the tabs back to stand up on a flat surface.)

More Puppets

You can find even more puppets in the Project Gallery under the Crafts Project Type, in the Party Goods category.

To create your own puppet designs, use the ready-made Templates for Puppets design. Add your own pictures to the puppet templates, and then print, cut, tape, and use.

Stickers

PrintMaster includes nine ready-made sticker designs, such as the one shown in Figure 11.5. These stickers can be printed on standard label sheets.

Even though a single sticker appears on your screen, when you choose to print a ready-made sticker, you print an entire page of stickers—and the changes you make to the single sticker are applied to all the stickers you print out. Before you print the stickers, however, you need to tell PrintMaster what types of label sheets you're using. Choose the Edit menu and select Choose Label Type. When the Choose a Label Type dialog box appears, select your labels from the list. After you select a label type, the label design is automatically resized to fit on your specific labels. Insert the label sheets in your printer and you're ready to print!

FIG. 11.5

A sheet of stickers, ready for printing.

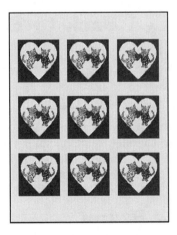

You can also create a sticker from scratch, by going to the Hub and clicking the Brand New button. When the New Project dialog box appears, select Sticker and click Next. When the Choose a Label Type dialog box appears, select your labels and click Finish. A "sheet" of blank labels now appears in the Design Workspace; choose one of the labels as your master sticker, and then add graphics or text to create your sticker.

After the master sticker is created, select all the elements on that label and copy them to the other labels on your page. After all the labels are filled with graphics, insert the sheet of labels into your printer and print your stickers!

Homework Helpers

Homework Helpers are ready-made PrintMaster projects that can be used as part of your children's school projects. To open a Homework Helper project, go to the Hub and select Ready-Made. When the Project Gallery appears, choose the Project Type list and select Homework Helpers. You can now choose from among the following categories of projects:

➤ Book report covers

➤ Dioramas

➤ Educational games

➤ Historical timelines

➤ Models

Many of these projects can be customized for your children's individual needs. Using a Homework Helper as part of a school project can send your child to the front of the class!

Book Report Covers

PrintMaster includes 20 different four-color book report covers, such as the one shown in Figure 11.6. You can print these covers as is (using a heavy paper stock, of course), or edit the text to add your child's name, class, and report title. To personalize a cover, edit the existing text, or add a new text box containing your child's name, class, and report title.

FIG. 11.6

A fun cover for a math project—personalize it with your child's name and class.

If you don't like any of the ready-made report covers, you can always create your own from scratch. The easiest way to do this is to open a Brand New project with a Blank Page, and then add your own picture and text items.

Dioramas

A diorama is a pyramid-shaped 3D object that presents a particular topic or theme across all its sides, as shown in Figure 11.7. PrintMaster includes eight different ready-made dioramas, ranging from A Desert Still Life to Western Town Twilight.

FIG. 11.7

This is what a diorama looks like when completed.

When you view a diorama onscreen, it looks a little confusing. That's because it prints out flat and then gets folded up into its final shape. When you print your diorama, make sure you print both pages—because the second page includes the assembly instructions!

You actually need to print four copies of your diorama (one for each of the four sides). Print your diorama on heavy paper or card stock, and then fold and assemble according to instructions. The results are impressive!

Educational Games

PrintMaster includes a few dozen educational games in the Homework Helper section. (Note that the 26 Alphabet Pockets are all part of a single game.) Most are board or maze games with an educational slant, such as How About Dem Bones?, Louisville Sluggers, and Wall-to-Wall Mathematics. Just select the game you want, print on the heaviest paper or card stock you can find, and get ready to play!

Make It Sturdy!

To make sure these game boards hold up under heavy use, paste the printed project onto a heavy piece of cardboard or wood, and then either laminate it or wrap it in clear wrapping tape.

Historical Timelines

PrintMaster provides seven different timelines you can print as banners and hang on your children's walls. These timelines—which are 2–3 feet long, when printed!—present the history of a specific topic. PrintMaster has timelines for Dinosaur Developments (see Figure 11.8), Scientific Inventions, the Seven Ancient Wonders of the World, U.S History Highlights, U.S. Presidents, Volcanic Eruptions Around the World, and World Civilization Events. Because these are extra-wide projects, you'll need to print on multiple sheets and then tape them together to complete the full banner.

FIG. 11.8

Hang the history of dinosaurs on your wall—this project is three sheets long!

Models

PrintMaster's models are three-dimensional projects, much like dioramas. Some of these projects (such as the one in Figure 11.9) are complex, and require a lot of precise cutting, folding, and assembling (along the lines of "insert tab A into slot B"). The results, however, are outstanding—especially projects such as A Castle Proud, Spanish Mission, and Stately Capitol.

FIG. 11.9

It takes some time to construct, but the Stately Capitol model will really impress your friends!

Other Fun Projects

Outside of Fun for Kids and Homework Helpers, PrintMaster includes several other general projects that your kids can have a lot of fun with. These projects—from banners to T-shirts—can often be printed as is, without much work involved.

Banners

PrintMaster includes over 300 different ready-made banners, in the following categories:

➤ Business
➤ Education

➤ Events

➤ Home

➤ Occasions

➤ Sports

Most of the kid-friendly banners are located in the Education category (under Primary and Secondary) and the Home category (under Children). There are also some neat banners in the Occasions category (under Birthday, Congratulations, Holidays, and Party) and the Sports category (under both Individual and Team). Figure 11.10 shows one of the more popular children's banners.

FIG. 11.10

An occasion worthy of a banner—school's out!

Banners are easy projects to complete. Just go to the Hub and select Ready-Made to display the Project Gallery. Select Banners as the Project Type, select a Category, and then select a specific banner. You can print the banner as is, or (in some cases) edit the text to include specific names.

When you print a banner, remember that you're printing a project that is very large. You'll have to print on multiple sheets of paper, and then tape them together to complete the full banner. Make sure that when the Print dialog box appears, you have All Tiles selected from the Which Tiles button. You can also choose to print the banner a little smaller by clicking the Output Size button and choosing a scale less than 100%.

Hats

Here's something fun—use PrintMaster to make hilarious paper hats! Just go to the Hub, click Brand New, select Craft from the New Project dialog box, and then click the Next button. When the Choose a Craft Type dialog box appears, select either Hat 1 (a cone-type "dunce" hat) or Hat 2 (a wide-billed golf hat, shown in Figure 11.11). When the project appears in the Design Workspace, either color the hat or add your own graphics or text. Make sure you print it on heavy paper or card stock, and then cut and fold it—and put in on your head!

FIG. 11.11

A project that's both fun and functional—a golf hat!

Ready-Made Hats

PrintMaster includes a handful of ready-made hats—including a King's Crown Hat and a St. Patrick's Hat—in the Project Gallery, under the Crafts Project Type in the Party Goods Category.

Photo Projects

PrintMaster's photo projects aren't just for adults. Kids can have lots of fun creating photo albums and novelty cards and posters using your own photos.

You access PrintMaster's photo projects by selecting Ready-Made from the Hub, and then choosing the Photo Projects Project Type from the Project Gallery. Here, you have your choice of five different types of projects:

➤ **Collages and Novelties.** In these projects, such as the one shown in Figure 11.12, you insert a photo of a face into a premade background on a card or poster. In many cases, you can also add your own funny text to accompany the picture.

FIG. 11.12
Hey! I'm the Mona Lisa*!*

➤ **Easy Prints.** These are essentially "thumbnails" of a single photo, printed several to a page.
➤ **Holidays.** These projects are much like the Collages and Novelties projects, but with holiday themes.
➤ **Occasions.** More novelty cards and posters.
➤ **Photo Album Pages.** Create your own personal photo albums.

141

To add your own photos to a photo project, choose the Add menu and select Picture from Disk. When the Open Picture from Disk dialog box appears, locate the file you want to open, and then click Open. Your photo now appears in the Design Workspace. Just move it into position and edit it to make it fit the open space in the photo project. When you have the fit right, make sure the photo is selected, choose the Arrange menu, select Layer, and then select Send to Back. This effectively "crops" your picture to fit in the "cutout" in the project.

Make the Picture Fit

You might have to crop and resize your pictures to make them fit in any given photo project. See Chapter 8, "Better Pictures and Photographs," to learn how to use Photo Workshop and other PrintMaster tools to edit and manage your photo files.

Posters

PrintMaster includes more than 350 ready-made posters, many of which your kids will get a kick out of. PrintMaster includes posters in the following categories:

➤ Business

➤ Events

➤ Home

➤ Occasions

➤ Sports

Most of the posters for kids are located in the Home category, under Children. You should also take a look at the posters in the Events category (under Education and General), the Occasions category (under Birthday, Congratulations, Graduation, Holidays, and Party), and the Sports category (under both Individual and Team). Figure 11.13 shows a cool children's poster.

It's easy to complete a poster project. Just go to the Hub and select Ready-Made to display the Project Gallery. Select Posters as the Project Type, select a Category, and then select a specific poster. You can print the poster as is, or (in some cases) edit the text or graphics.

Some posters are small enough to print on a single page. Others require multiple-sheet printing. In fact, you can size your poster to be as big as you want—just click the Output Size button in the Print dialog box and enter the desired dimensions or scale.

FIG. 11.13
*A poster for the door of
every teenager's room!*

Poster or Banner?

A poster is typically a rectangular project, in either portrait or land-scape orientation, where the longer side is less than two times the length of the shorter side. A banner, on the other hand, is a project where the length exceeds the height by three times or more.

Puzzles

If you like jigsaw puzzles, you'll really like PrintMaster's puzzle projects. You can create a 9-piece, 20-piece, or 42-piece jigsaw puzzle—with any picture of your choosing!

Start from the Hub and select Brand New. When the New Project dialog box appears, select Craft and click Next. When the Choose a Craft Type dialog box appears, select one of the three Puzzle options and click Finish.

The puzzle template now appears in the Design Workspace. Click the Art Gallery to select a picture for your puzzle, and then resize the picture to fit the entire puzzle. When the artwork is sized correctly, select the picture, choose the Arrange menu, select Layer, and then select Send to Back. This places the puzzle template on top of the graphic—as shown in Figure 11.14—so you can easily cut out the individual puzzle pieces.

When you print the puzzle, use heavy paper or card stock. Then *carefully* cut out the individual puzzle pieces, according to the template. Now, you can shuffle the pieces and start assembling your new jigsaw puzzle!

FIG. 11.14

*Turn any picture into a
42-piece jigsaw puzzle!*

More Puzzles

You can find even more puzzle templates—as well as some ready-made
picture puzzles—in the Project Gallery under the Crafts Project Type,
in the Puzzles category.

T-Shirts

Using iron-on transfers, you can use PrintMaster to create T-shirts with your own personalized images. (Remember that all text and pictures must be printed *backward* to
come out frontward on your T-shirt!)

Ready-Made T-Shirts

PrintMaster includes a variety of ready-made T-shirt designs in the
Project Gallery, under the Crafts Project Type in the T-Shirts Category.

Start from the Hub and select Brand New. When the New Project dialog box appears,
select Craft and click Next. When the Choose a Craft Type dialog box appears, select
T-Shirt and click Finish.

You now see a blank page in the Design Workspace. Add whatever text or pictures
you want, and then click the Print button. When the Print dialog box appears, check

Print Reversed for Iron-On Transfer Paper, and then click Print. (Make sure you have the iron-on transfer loaded into your printer, of course!) After the transfer is printed, iron it onto your favorite blank T-shirt, and you're ready to wear your latest project!

Reverse *Any* Project

You don't have to start with a T-shirt project to make a T-shirt. You can turn virtually any PrintMaster project into an iron-transfer for a T-shirt by checking the Print Reversed for Iron-On Transfer Paper option in the Print dialog box.

In the Next Chapter...

In this chapter, you learned how to create some fun projects for kids. In the next chapter, you'll see some projects for the entire family—including PrintMaster 8.0's new Kitchen Crafts!

Chapter 12

Projects for the Hon

PrintMaster includes a variety of projects you can use around the house—both fun and practical projects you can complete with a minimum of fuss and muss. Whether you need personal stationery, holiday greeting cards, or an origami fish, it's easy to make with PrintMaster!

Crafts

PrintMaster includes a variety of ready-made craft projects, in a variety of categories, including

> ➤ **Cut-Out Cards.** Choose from four odd-sized cards, including a Do Not Disturb sign, a triangular gift tag, and a pop-up Valentine's Day card. Print these on heavy paper or card stock, and then cut, fold, and assemble according to the instructions.

> ➤ **Gift Bags & Boxes.** Choose from 40 different bags and boxes. You'll need to print these on the appropriate paper or card stock, then cut, fold, and assemble as directed.

> ➤ **Origami.** Choose from 26 different three-dimensional projects, of varying degrees of difficulty. (See Figure 12.1 for one example.) You'll print these flat, of course, but then cut and fold according to instructions.

➤ **Ornaments.** Choose from 29 three-dimensional Christmas ornaments. Print on heavy paper or card stock, and then cut, fold, and assemble as instructed—and hang from your favorite tree!

➤ **Party Goods.** Choose from 15 finger puppets (under the Games heading), 6 hats, and 7 place cards.

Matching Party Sets

You can find hundreds of additional party projects in the Project Gallery under the Matching Sets Project Type. When you select Matching Sets projects, you get the same design and graphics for all your party items—including cards, invitations, nametags, banners, and posters.

➤ **Puzzles.** Choose from 12 different jigsaw puzzle projects and templates. Make sure you print these on heavy paper or card stock, and then cut out the individual puzzle pieces as precisely as possible!

➤ **Self-Mailing.** Choose from 17 self-mailing invitations. Just print, cut, and fold to create a mailing piece that doesn't need an envelope—you can even personalize with your own text!

➤ **T-Shirts.** Choose from 47 designs you can print (reversed) on iron-on transfer paper—then iron onto your favorite T-shirt!

➤ **Workshop.** Choose from over 200 three-dimensional models. You can create a variety of different items, including miniature furniture (great for mocking up new house designs), dollhouses, animals, paper airplanes, cars (see Figure 12.2), and paper dolls. Just print (on heavy paper or card stock), cut, fold, and assemble according to the individual instructions.

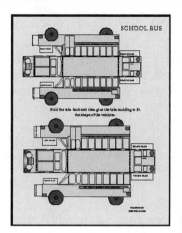

FIG. 12.2
Make a paper school bus with Workshop crafts.

You can access all of these projects by selecting Ready-Made from the Hub, and then selecting the Crafts Category in the Project Gallery.

Kitchen Crafts

New in PrintMaster 8.0 are a variety of Kitchen Crafts, including

➤ **Accordion Folders.** Choose from five types of folders you can use to hold recipe cards, postage stamps, and personal notes.

➤ **Bottle Labels.** Choose from five individual gift labels (such as the one shown in Figure 12.3) to hang from the necks of wine bottles and similar gifts.

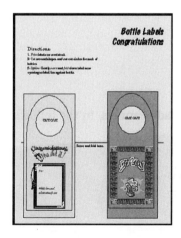

FIG. 12.3
Hang this label from a bottle of wine—and you've created a perfect gift!

➤ **Stencils.** Choose from three different sheet stencils for cake decorating, painting, or other creative uses.

➤ **Switchplate Covers.** Choose from nine decorative covers for one- and two-switch wall plates. You print these double-sided, with the instructions and template on one side, and the pattern on the other—then, you glue the patterned cover to your existing switchplate.

You can access the Kitchen Crafts projects by selecting Ready-Made from the Hub, and then selecting the Kitchen Crafts Category in the Project Gallery.

Crafts from Scratch

You can also create a variety of craft projects from scratch. Just select Brand New from the Hub, and then select one of the crafts-oriented options from the New Project dialog box—including Poster, Banner, Calendar, Certificate, Sticker, or T-Shirt. If you select the Craft option in the New Project dialog box, you can choose from the following interesting projects:

➤ Bag

➤ Basket

➤ Box

➤ Centerpiece

➤ Doorhanger

➤ Frame

➤ Hat (two variations)

➤ Mask

➤ Puzzle (three variations)

Banners

Choose from over 300 different rea

➤ Business

➤ Education

➤ Events

➤ Home

➤ Occasions

➤ Sports

150

Banners are easy projects to complete. Just go to the Hub and select Ready-Made to display the Project Gallery. Select Banners as the Project Type, select a Category, and then select a specific banner. (See Figure 12.4 for an example.) You can print the banner as is, or (in some cases) edit the text to include specific names.

FIG. 12.4

One of PrintMaster's 300 ready-made banners—this one prints across three sheets of paper.

You can also create a blank banner on which you can place your own text and graphics. Go to the Hub and select Brand New; when the New Project dialog box appears, select Banner, and then click Finish. Edit the "banner" text or add your own graphics to create a custom banner!

Banners Are BIG!

Because most banners are at least two feet wide, you'll have to print on multiple sheets of paper, and then tape them together to complete the full banner. Make sure that when the Print dialog box appears, you have All Tiles selected from the Which Tiles button. You can also choose to print the banner a little smaller by clicking the Output Size button and choosing a scale less than 100%.

Calendars

PrintMaster includes almost 200 different types of ready-made calendars. You can choose from weekly calendars, monthly calendars, yearly calendars, calendars with pictures of bunnies, calendars with pictures of flowers, calendars with no pictures at all—in short, just about any kind of calendar you can imagine!

To choose a calendar, go to the Hub and select Ready-Made; when the Project Gallery appears, select Calendars as the Project Type. After you select a specific calendar (like the one in Figure 12.5), it's time to edit the calendar. You can edit any specific day in the calendar—just right-click the day, and choose from one of the available options on the pop-up menu. In most cases, you can edit the text, color, and picture for each individual date.

FIG. 12.5

Personalize your own calendar by editing individual dates.

Many of these calendars are multiple-page projects—with a cover page and pages for each month or week. Make sure you print out the entire calendar when you're ready to print.

Check the Year...

Make sure you select a calendar for the current year—and note that PrintMaster includes several calendars for years past! (You probably don't want to print a 1996 calendar at the end of 1999...)

You can also create your own calendars from scratch. Go to the Hub and select Brand New; when the New Project dialog box appears, select Calendar, and then click the Next button. When the Calendar Type dialog box appears, select either Yearly, Monthly, or Weekly, and then click Next. When the Orientation dialog box appears, select either a Tall or Wide calendar, and then click Next. When the Picture Placement dialog box appears, choose whether or not to add a picture, and if so, where (Above, To Side, or On the Same Page), and then click Next. When the Calendar Date dialog box appears, select the correct time period for your calendar, and then click Finish. When the completed calendar appears in the Design Workspace, add your own colors and graphics, and then print!

Cards

PrintMaster lets you create several different types of cards. From the Project Type list in the Project Gallery, you can select from the following:

➤ **Cards, Half-Fold.** Choose from over 2,000 cards that print on a single sheet folded once. (See Figure 12.6 for a sample.)

➤ **Cards, Quarter-Fold.** Choose from more than 2,500 cards that print on a single sheet folded twice (in quarters).

➤ **Note Cards.** Choose from more than 150 single-sided cards that are perfect for short, personalized notes.

➤ **Postcards.** Choose from 46 different two-sided postcards. Make sure you choose the Edit menu and select Choose Postcard Type to select the type of card you're using. (When you click the Print button, you can choose to print the front, back, or both sides of your cards.)

FIG. 12.6

Use PrintMaster to make your own custom Christmas cards!

If you're like most PrintMaster users, you'll print a lot of cards. When you're printing half-fold or quarter-fold cards, you can choose from cards in dozens of different categories, from Anniversary, Birthday, and Christmas to Graduation, Secretary's Day, and Wedding. You can customize the cards as you want, adding your own personal text and your preferred pictures and photographs. Make sure you print the cards on good card stock, and your recipients will think you spent big bucks to print custom cards just for them!

If you want to create truly customized cards, you have two options. You can go to the Hub and select With Help, and then use the With Help Designer to create a new Greeting Card. Or you can go to the Hub and select Brand New, and then select either Quarter-Fold Card, Half-Fold Card, Note Card, or Post Card. In either case, you can add your own graphics and text to make a totally unique set of cards.

Get Sentimental

If you're creating a new card and you're not quite sure what to say, use PrintMaster's prewritten Sentiments. As explained in Chapter 10, "Better Projects with PrintMaster's Special Tools," the Sentiment Gallery lets you add preselected front and inside messages to your greeting cards. Start with either a blank card, or a ready-made card with the default text deleted, and then click the Sentiment Gallery button in the Format toolbar. When the Sentiment Gallery appears, browse through the different categories, select a front/back sentiment, and then click the Select button. The sentiment text is added to the front and inside of your card; you can then reposition, resize, and format the text to match the rest of your card.

Certificates

PrintMaster includes 145 ready-made certificates you can use to reward and motivate your friends, colleagues, and family. Go to the Hub and select Ready-Made; when the Project Gallery appears, pull down the Project Type list and select Certificates. From here, you can choose from four different categories:

➤ Achievements (see Figure 12.7)

➤ Awards

➤ Coupons (printed several to a sheet)

➤ Motivational

FIG. 12.7

A certificate of achievement, suitable for framing.

You can also create blank certificates and customize them for your specific needs. Go to the Hub and select Brand New; when the New Project dialog box appears, select Certificate, and click Next. When the Orientation dialog box appears, choose from Tall or Wide, and then click Finish. You're now presented with a blank page; use the Art Gallery to insert pictures and artwork, and then add your own text. The result: a custom certificate, suitable for framing!

Letterhead

With PrintMaster, you can choose from over 200 different types of letterhead for your personal correspondence. Just go to the Hub and select Ready-Made; when the Project Gallery appears, pull down the Project Type list and select Letterhead. You'll probably want to skip the Business category, but there are a lot of attractive designs in the Education, Personal, Spiritual, and Sports categories. Figure 12.8 shows just one of the many designs you can choose from.

FIG. 12.8

You don't need to send letters on plain white paper anymore—PrintMaster lets you design your own personal letterhead!

You can also design your own letterhead with either the With Help Designer or from scratch with the Brand New option. To use the With Help Designer, go to the Hub and select With Help; when the With Help dialog box appears, select Letterhead, click Next, and follow the onscreen instructions. To design new letterhead from scratch, go to the Hub, select Brand New, and then select Letterhead from the New Project dialog box. When you click Next, select whether you want to print Tall or Wide, and then click Finish. When the blank letterhead appears in the Design Workspace, add your own graphics and text to create truly custom letterhead.

Keep It Light—With Room to Write

Remember, you're designing the background for your personal letters, not a fancy-schmancy poster. Keep the background light enough to write on, and leave enough space in the center for a normal letter!

Envelopes

PrintMaster includes almost 300 different envelope designs. All you have to do is add the recipient's address and your return address, and you have a personalized envelope to use with your own custom stationery.

Just go to the Hub and select Ready-Made; when the Project Gallery appears, choose the Project Type list and select Envelopes. You can choose from several different types of envelopes—Business, Education, Occasions, Personal, Spiritual, and Sports. When the selected envelope appears in the Design Workspace, enter your custom text, and click the Print button.

Pick the Right Envelope

Before you get too involved with designing your envelope, you need to tell PrintMaster what size envelope you'll be printing. To do this, choose the Edit menu, select Choose an Envelope Type, and select which envelope you're using.

When the Print dialog box appears, there's one new option you have to deal with—the Envelope Feed option. When you click the Envelope Feed button, you display the Envelope Feed dialog box (shown in Figure 12.9); select the option that best describes how you feed envelopes into your printer, and then click OK.

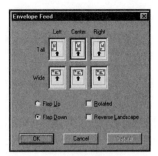

FIG. 12.9
Choose how envelopes are fed into your printer—tall, wide, flush right, flush left, centered, flap up, or flap down.

Print to a Mailing List

You can print multiple envelopes at one time, addressed to different recipients in a personalized mailing list. To do this, you need to add a Mail Merge Field (within a Text Box). To learn more about merge fields and mailing list printing, see Chapter 10.

PrintMaster also lets you design your own envelopes from scratch. Go to the Hub, select Brand New, and then select Envelopes from the New Project dialog box. When you click Next, choose the size of envelope you want to print, and then click Finish. When the blank envelope appears in the Design Workspace, add graphics and text to your personal taste.

Garlands

PrintMaster includes seven different tabletop decorations you can print, cut, and fold to shape. Go to the Hub, select Ready-Made, and then pull down the Project Gallery's Project Type list and select Garlands. Print these garlands on card stock, and stand them up to decorate your room for a specific occasion.

Invitations

Whatever the occasion, you can use PrintMaster to print personalized invitations. Just go to the Hub and select Ready-Made; when the Project Gallery appears, pull down the Project Type list and select Invitations. PrintMaster provides 200 different invitations for holidays and other occasions. When you select an invitation (like the one in Figure 12.10), it appears in the Design Workspace, ready to be edited or printed as is. Naturally, you want to print your invitations on heavy paper or card stock.

FIG. 12.10

You're invited to a party—thanks to PrintMaster's Invitations!

Many invitations are multiple-sided. For example, you may have a front, inside, and back to the invitation. To switch from one side to another in the Design Workspace, use the View Side section of the Status Bar; the forward and backward arrows switch from one side to another of your invitation.

When it's time to print your invitation, you may have to use PrintMaster's double-sided printing option. (In other cases, the entire invitation fits one side of a sheet—you just have to fold it to create the invitation.) To set up your printer for double-sided printing, see Chapter 4, "Print Your Projects." After you've printed the first side of the project, you are prompted to reinsert the page to print the second side; follow the onscreen instructions to complete the printing.

More Invitations in Matching Sets

If you want to coordinate invitations with other party items, select the Matching Sets Project Type in the Project Gallery. There, you can choose from matching invitations, nametags, cards, posters, banners, and thank-you notes.

Labels

PrintMaster lets you create all different types of labels for various uses around your home. Not only can you create standard mailing (address, return, and shipping) labels, you can also create:

➤ Labels for audio and videotapes (see Figure 12.11)

➤ Labels to personalize your books

➤ Labels for computer floppy disks

➤ Labels for bottles and other household goods

➤ Nametags and other personal labels

➤ Rotary cards for Rolodex files

FIG. 12.11

Use PrintMaster to create professional-looking labels for your videotape collection.

Just go to the Hub and select Ready-Made, and when the Project Gallery appears, select Labels from the Project Type list. Select the label you want, insert your own personal information, and print.

When you print labels, you need to tell PrintMaster what kind of label sheets you're using. To do this, choose the Edit menu and select Choose Label Type. When the Choose a Label Type dialog box appears, select the labels you're using and click OK.

You Don't Have to Use the Whole Sheet

If you want to print only a few labels from a larger sheet, click the Starting Label button in the Print dialog box and select which label on the sheet you're starting with.

Photo Albums

PrintMaster includes several different types of photo projects. Some of the more fun projects (collages and novelties) were described in Chapter 11, "Projects for Kids." Chapter 8 describes photo projects you can complete with Photo Workshop and Photo Organizer. Here, we'll look exclusively at PrintMaster's ready-made photo album projects.

Start by going to the Hub and selecting Ready-Made. When the Project Gallery appears, select Photo Projects from the Project Type list, and then select Photo Album Pages from the Category list. You can now select from 27 different types of photo albums, such as the vacation album shown in Figure 12.12.

FIG. 12.12

Create your own vacation photo album with PrintMaster!

Most photo album projects have a cover page and a single interior page. You can add more interior pages by choosing the Add menu and selecting Pages; when the Add Pages dialog box appears, select the number of pages to add, and check the After Current Page option. Also check the Add Copies of Page option, and enter **2** in the corresponding box. Click OK, and PrintMaster adds more photo pages to your album.

To add photos to your album, first delete the "place photo here" text boxes, and then choose the Add menu and select Picture from Disk. Select the picture to add from the Open Picture from Disk dialog box, and click Open. When the picture appears on your page, move it, resize it, and rotate it (in some cases) to fit in the proper place.

Edit Your Photos

To edit a photo you've placed in a project, select the photo and then click the Photo Workshop button in the Format toolbar. When you select any option from the pop-up menu, Photo Workshop launches, with your picture loaded and ready for editing. After you're done editing, click OK to place the newly edited picture back in your project.

Posters

You can use PrintMaster to decorate your walls with colorful posters. PrintMaster includes ready-made posters in five major categories: Business, Events, Home, Occasions, and Sports.

To select a ready-made poster, go to the Hub and select Ready-Made. When the Project Gallery appears, select Posters from the Project Type list, select a Category, and then select a specific poster. You can print the poster as is, or (in some cases) edit the text or graphics. Figure 12.13 displays one of the more than 350 ready-made posters included with PrintMaster.

FIG. 12.13

Use PrintMaster to create your garage sale posters.

You can also create posters with the With Help Designer and the Brand New functions. To use the With Help Designer, go to the Hub and select With Help; when the With Help dialog box appears, select Poster, click Next, and follow the onscreen instructions. To design a new poster from scratch, go to the Hub, select Brand New, and then select Poster from the New Project dialog box. When you click Next, select whether you want a Tall or Wide poster, and click Finish. When the blank poster appears in the Design Workspace, add your own graphics and text to create something you are proud to hang on your wall.

Size to Fit

You can size any poster to be as big as you want. When the Print dialog box appears, click the Output Size button and enter the desired dimensions or scale. Remember, however, if you size your picture really big, you'll have to print on multiple sheets, and then tape them together to form the complete poster.

In the Next Chapter...

In this chapter, you learned how to create projects for your home. In the next chapter, you'll learn how to create projects for a small or home-based business—including newsletters and brochures!

Chapter 13

Projects for Small and Home-Based Businesses

PrintMaster isn't just for crafts and hobbies—it can also create professional projects you can use in your small business or home-based business. Whether you need business cards or a multiple-page newsletter, use PrintMaster to get your business up and running!

Business Essentials

PrintMaster includes projects to let you create all the essential items you need to launch any type of small business—including business cards, letterhead, envelopes, forms, fax cover sheets, and brochures. You can choose from hundreds of ready-made projects, or design your own from scratch or from the With Help Designer.

When you create your business essentials, remember to use a design that reflects the tone and identity of your individual business. You can incorporate your own logo into any design, of course—and if you do, make sure the fonts used in the project match the design of your logo.

You'll also want to replicate a single design across all your business essentials. So, after you create your business cards, for example, cut and paste the graphics and text from there into your other projects (and resize and edit appropriately, of course).

Matching Letters and Envelopes—In Matching Sets

The easiest way for all your business essentials to share the same design is to use PrintMaster's Matching Sets feature. From the Project Gallery, select Matching Sets from the Project Type list, and then select Business from the Category list. PrintMaster now displays a half-dozen master designs for envelopes, letterhead, business cards, brochures, and fax cover sheets. You still open each project individually, but all the projects within a design "family" share the same look and feel.

Business Cards

PrintMaster provides more than 200 ready-made business card designs. To view them, go to the Hub and select Ready-Made. When the Project Gallery appears, select Business Cards from the Project Type list, and then choose from one of five different categories of cards: Business, Education, Personal, Spiritual, and Sports.

When you open a business card project, such as the one shown in Figure 13.1, your specific business information is automatically inserted in the appropriate fields. (This assumes, of course, that you filled out PrintMaster's Sender Information; if you haven't, choose the Tools menu and select Sender Information now.) You can edit any of this information, of course; for example, you may want to shrink the standard address and phone number text a bit and add your email and Web page addresses.

FIG. 13.1

One of PrintMaster's ready-made business cards, with your business name, address, and phone number automatically added.

The Molehill Group

THE RECYCLE MAN

1234 Circle Drive Road
Carmel, IN 46032
317-555-5555

You'll probably also want to replace the "stock" logo with your own company's logo. You'll need to delete PrintMaster's logo graphic, and insert your own logo file. (Just choose the Add menu and select Picture from Disk.) Resize or edit your logo as needed. If necessary, you can also edit the existing text on the card to change its font, size, attributes, or color.

The result—seen in Figure 13.2—is a custom-made card for your business, based on one of PrintMaster's professional ready-made designs.

FIG. 13.2

The same ready-made design, customized with your business logo, email, Web page addresses, and slogan—ready to print!

[You] can also design a business card from scratch. From the Hub, select [and] when the New Project dialog box appears, select Business Card and [th]en the Orientation dialog box appears, select Tall or Wide, and then [yo]u now see a blank business card; add your logo and text in your own [...]'re ready to print.

Impressive Business Cards

[...] print your business cards on heavy-duty card stock to pro-
[...] degree of durability. You can find special card stocks at most office supply stores (including some that come perforated for easy separation); think about using a textured or color stock to give your cards some individuality.

Letterhead

PrintMaster includes over 100 different ready-made letterhead designs; most of these designs mirror the ready-made business card designs. Go to the Hub and select Ready-Made, and when the Project Gallery appears, choose the Project Type list and select Letterhead. Most of the designs you'll be interested in are in the Business category. Figure 13.3 shows just one of the many designs you can choose from.

FIG. 13.3

You'll find professional letterhead designs in the ready-made Project Gallery.

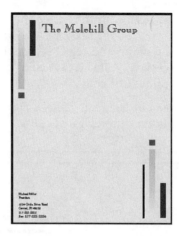

Naturally, you'll want to use your own logo, and add any business-specific text to the standard address and phone number information. You'll most certainly want to add your email address, and perhaps a Web site address and cell phone number. To make all this fit, you'll probably have to reduce the size of or rearrange the existing text.

You can also design your own letterhead with either the With Help Designer or from scratch with the Brand New option. To use the With Help Designer, go to the Hub and select With Help; when the With Help dialog box appears, select Letterhead, click Next, and follow the onscreen instructions. To design new letterhead from scratch, go to the Hub, select Brand New, and then choose Letterhead from the New Project dialog box. When you click Next, select whether you want to print Tall or Wide, and then click Finish. When the blank letterhead appears in the Design Workspace, add your own logo and text.

Envelopes

When you select Envelopes from the Project Type list in the Project Gallery, you can choose from over 100 different business envelope designs. Again, most of these designs (such as the one in Figure 13.4) mirror similar ready-made business card and letterhead designs. Depending on the size of your logo, you may or may not want to add it to the return section of the envelope. Just remember that the upper-left section of the envelope can't be *too* big!

Pick the Right Envelope

Before you get too involved with designing your envelope, you need to tell PrintMaster what size envelope you'll be printing. To do this, choose the Edit menu, select Choose an Envelope Type, and select which envelope you're using.

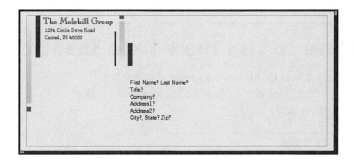

FIG. 13.4

Customize a ready-made envelope design for your own particular business.

You can also design your own business envelopes from scratch. Go to the Hub, select Brand New, and then select Envelopes from the New Project dialog box. When you click Next, choose the size of envelope you want to print, and click Finish. When the blank envelope appears in the Design Workspace, add your logo and text in your own custom design.

When it's time to print your envelopes, you have to select the proper type of Envelope Feed. When you click the Envelope Feed button, you display the Envelope Feed dialog box; select the option that best describes how you feed envelopes into your printer, and click OK.

Preparing a Business Mailing

You can use PrintMaster to send a mass mailing to multiple names in your Address Book. You'll need to add a Mail Merge Field to a text block in the recipient section of your envelope, click the Merge Names button in the Print dialog box, and select the desired recipients from your Address Book. See Chapter 10, "Better Projects with PrintMaster's Special Tools," for more information about PrintMaster's mail merge function.

Labels

If you're mailing oversized envelopes or shipping larger boxes, you can use PrintMaster to create various types of shipping labels. Just go to the Hub and select Ready-Made, and then when the Project Gallery appears, select Labels from the Project Type list. You'll probably want to choose from the labels in the Address, Return, and Shipping categories, and then edit with your logo and business address.

When you print labels, you need to tell PrintMaster what kind of label sheets you're using. To do this, choose the Edit menu and select Choose Label Type. When the Choose a Label Type dialog box appears, select the labels you're using and click OK.

You Don't Have to Use the Whole Sheet

If you want to print only a few labels from a larger sheet, click the Starting Label button in the Print dialog box and select which label on the sheet you're starting with.

Fax Cover Sheets

PrintMaster includes close to 200 fax cover sheet designs, most of which mirror the ready-made business card, letterhead, and envelope designs. Just go to the Project Gallery and select Fax Cover Sheets from the Project Type list. Pick a design, add your own logo and text information, and you're ready to print—and then fax!

Simplify the Design

Because fax machines work in black and white only, one can question why you would want to use a *color* fax cover sheet. In fact, it's a pretty dumb idea to use a color cover sheet for a black-and-white fax—anything that isn't black and white can become quite muddy and unreadable at the other end of the fax transmission. You'll get better results if you edit the color graphics in the cover sheet to black and white *before* you send the fax. While you're at it, work on simplifying all aspects of the cover sheet. Definitely remove any overall back-ground graphics, and think about enlarging the text a tad. Just remember that faxing a document results in *lower print-quality output*, because things tend to smear and pixelate. Big and simple is the way to go when designing documents for faxing purposes.

You can also design your own fax forms from scratch. Just go to the Hub, select Brand New, select Fax Cover from the New Project dialog box, and click Next. After you select the orientation, you'll have a blank page, on which you can place your logo and other information.

Forms

You can also use PrintMaster to create invoices and order forms for your business. Start at the Hub and select Ready-Made; when the Project Gallery appears, choose the Project Type list and select Forms. PrintMaster includes various types of ready-made forms, such as the one shown in Figure 13.5. Pick the one that best meets your business needs, and then edit it to include your logo and phone/address information—as well as your specific terms.

FIG. 13.5

Use PrintMaster to create custom invoices and purchase orders.

Brochures and Flyers

Most brochures print on a single sheet of paper (double-sided, in most instances), and then fold to present the illusion of multiple pages (called *panels*). A brochure that folds once is a *double-fold* brochure and has four panels (two per side); one that has three folds is a *tri-fold* brochure with six panels (three per side).

PrintMaster includes over 150 ready-made brochures in four different categories—Business, Education, Events, and Sports. Just select Brochures & Flyers from the Project Gallery's Project Type list to see the available selections.

When the selected brochure appears in the Design Workspace (see Figure 13.6), you see the basic design with so-called "Greek" text used for placement purposes only. Replace the Greek text with your own text, and then add your own logo and other information. To view the other side of the brochure, click the front or back arrow in the View Side section of the Status Bar.

FIG. 13.6

A ready-made brochure, ready for editing; replace the "Greek" text with real text.

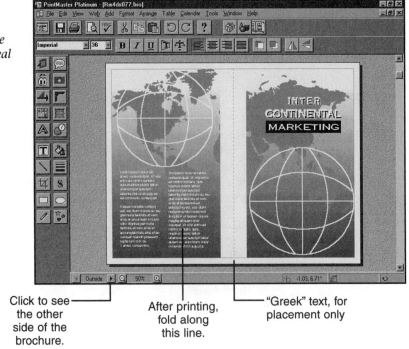

Click to see the other side of the brochure.

After printing, fold along this line.

"Greek" text, for placement only

You can also create a brochure from scratch when you select Brand New from the Hub. When the New Project dialog box appears, select Brochure and click Next. When the Orientation dialog box appears, select the Orientation (Tall or Wide), and the number of Panels per side (2, 3, or 4). When you click Finish, a blank brochure is displayed, according to your specifications. Add your own graphics and text to create your own custom-designed brochure.

Before you print your brochure, make sure you've properly set up PrintMaster's double-sided print function. (Just choose the File menu and select Double-Sided Print Setup.) When you click the Print button, make sure the following options are checked: Print Range: Both Sides, Double-Sided, and Print Instruction Page. Follow the instructions to print both sides of the brochure, and then fold accordingly.

Newsletters

Perhaps the most complex type of project you can create with PrintMaster is a newsletter. For that reason, the rest of this chapter is devoted to showing you, step-by-step, how to create a professional-looking newsletter.

Getting Started

PrintMaster includes over 150 ready-made newsletter designs, organized into Business, Education, Personal, Spiritual, and Sports categories. (Figure 13.7 shows one of the many ready-made newsletters.) To access these designs, select Ready-Made from the Hub, choose the Project Type list in the Project Gallery, and select Newsletters.

FIG. 13.7

Start with a ready-made newsletter design from the Project Gallery.

You can also use the With Help Designer to start your newsletter project. Just select With Help from the Hub, and then select Newsletters (and click Next) from the With Help dialog box. Choose the type of newsletter (Business, Educational, or Personal) and the desired style, and then select how many pages and whether you want a double-sided newsletter. Click Finish to display a blank newsletter that follows your specifications.

Finally, you can choose to create a newsletter completely from scratch. Go to the Hub, select Brand New, and when the New Project dialog box appears, select Newsletters and click Next. When the Orientation dialog box appears, select either Tall or Wide orientation, choose whether you're creating a Double-Sided newsletter, and then click Finish.

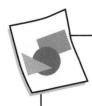

Use All the Tools

When you're creating a newsletter, you have the opportunity to use all the tools PrintMaster puts at your disposal. You can use the Headline tool to add a sophisticated headline; the Text Box tool to add new articles and text pieces; the Fill Color tool to shade selected text boxes; the Line tool to add horizontal rules between articles; the BorderPlus tool to add special borders around specific articles or columns; the Table tool to display selected information in rows and columns; the DrawPlus tool to add your own drawings; the Art Gallery to add various types of graphics; and the Photo Workshop tool to add photographs. Use whatever tools you need to create a professional-looking newsletter—quickly and easily!

Adding Pages

No matter how you start a newsletter, what you have in front of you is page one of what can (and probably will) be a multiple-page project. To add additional pages to the newsletter, choose the Add menu and select Pages. When the Add Pages dialog box appears, select how many pages you want to add, and whether you want to add the pages after or before the current page.

You can also choose to add blank pages, or copies of an existing page. The latter option is worth choosing if you've already created the *perfect* page design, and want to replicate it on later pages. If you do choose to add a copy of an existing page, you'll obviously want to replace the text (and possibly graphics) with new text.

To switch between pages of your newsletter, use the forward and backward buttons in the Page Selector section of the Status Bar (also called the View Sides section). You can also click the center of the Page Selector section to display a pop-up menu that provides more page navigation options.

Flowing Text

As explained in Chapter 9, "Better Text," you add text to your newsletter via text boxes. If you have a long article, chances are it will either flow to a second column or to another page. You make this happen by adding new text boxes, and *flowing* the text from one text box to another, by connecting the text boxes.

To connect two text boxes, click the Link button at the bottom of the first text box; your cursor becomes a *Text Flow* icon (with an "X" over it). Move the Text Flow icon over the second text box (you can link only to *empty* text boxes) and click your mouse button. Any excess text from the first text box now flows into the second text box. (Figure 13.8 shows text flowing from one text box to another.)

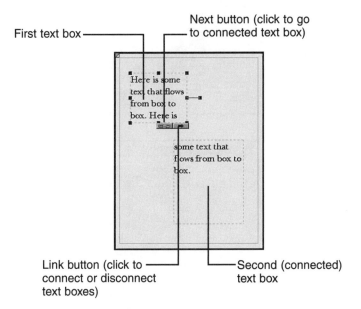

Next button (click to go to connected text box)

First text box

Link button (click to connect or disconnect text boxes)

Second (connected) text box

FIG. 13.8

Text flowing from column to column via connected text boxes.

To disconnect a text box, select both that text box (first) and then the previous text box to which it is connected. Click the Link button on the main text box and the flowed text disappears from the (now) previously connected text box.

Using a Master Page Design

Any newsletter project you create (whether Ready-Made, With Help, or Brand New) includes a blank *master page* that functions as a template for the entire newsletter. You use the master page to hold pictures, text, or other design elements that you want to appear on *all* the pages of your newsletter. These master elements appear as a common layer on all pages; when you print your newsletter, the master layer prints along with all the page-specific elements you've added.

You work on the master page separately from the individual newsletter pages. (You can't select master page elements from an individual page, for example.) To view and edit your master page, choose the View menu and select Go to Master Page. To return to an individual page, choose the View menu and select Return to Page. Figure 13.9 shows a complete newsletter page with both individual page elements; Figure 13.10 shows just the master page for that page.

Figure 13.9

A newsletter page with both individual and master elements.

FIG. 13.10

The master page behind the individual page.

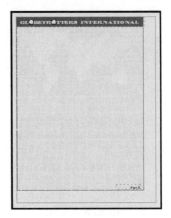

If your newsletter is double-sided, you actually have *two* master pages—left and right. Note that the front page of your newsletter is always a right page, and the back page is always a left page; one-sided newsletters have only a right master page. You can select different master design elements for your left and right pages.

If you have a page that you *don't* want to follow the master design, you can turn off the master page for that and other individual pages. This hides all master page elements for the select page(s), even though they remain on all other pages. To do this, go to the page you want to change, choose the View menu, and check Hide Master Page. To turn the master page back on, choose the View menu again and *uncheck* the Hide Master Page option.

Adding Page Numbers

To add page numbers to your newsletter, go to the master page, insert a text box, choose the Add menu, and select Add Page Number. (If you have a double-sided newsletter, repeat this procedure for both the left and right pages.) PrintMaster automatically adds the correct page number to each page—and adjusts the page numbering when you add or delete pages.

Ready to Print

You can print your newsletter on any type of paper. If you have a really complex newsletter, you should probably stick to a good grade of plain white paper. However, you might want to check out special bonds or colors to give your newsletter a unique look and feel.

If you're printing a double-sided newsletter, make sure the Double-Sided option is checked in the Print dialog box. You might also want to check the Print Instruction Page option, just in case you need help folding and assembling a multiple-page newsletter.

Setting Up Double-Sided Printing

To set up PrintMaster for double-sided printing, choose the File menu and select Double-Sided Print Setup. Follow the wizard's onscreen instructions to determine how your printer handles double-sided projects. (See Chapter 4, "Print Your Projects," for more information on double-sided printing.)

In the Next Chapter...

In this section, you learned how to create projects for your kids, your home, and your business. In the next section, you learn how to use PrintMaster on the Internet—for everything from email greeting cards to personal Web pages! Get started with Chapter 14, "Discover PrintMaster's Online Resources"—and progress from there.

PrintMaster
PART 4

Get Online:
How to Use
PrintMaster with
the Internet

Discover PrintMaster's Online Resources

The Learning Company (TLC) uses the Internet to provide additional resources and support for PrintMaster users. The PrintMaster Web site lets you chat with other users, order new products, download new artwork, and send email greeting cards. It's a great adjunct to the core PrintMaster product.

Setting PrintMaster's Online Preferences

Before you can go online with PrintMaster, you need to configure the program for your specific Internet connection. Begin by choosing PrintMaster's File menu and selecting Online Preferences. When the Online dialog box appears, select whether you're connecting via a Modem or a Direct Connection. (If you're connecting over a local area network at your office or school, you're using a Direct Connection.) If you're connecting via modem (and you probably are), select which connection you're using from the Dial-Up Connection list. If you're using a standard Windows connection, select Dial-Up Networking; if you're connecting via AOL, select America Online for Windows. Click OK when finished.

Windows Connections

To use PrintMaster on the Internet, you need to have already established an Internet connection, using a modem connected to an Internet service provider (ISP). PrintMaster doesn't offer Internet service—you have to obtain your own account with an ISP before you can access the PrintMaster Web site.

If you need to search for an ISP account—and have access to a computer connected to the Internet—you can search The List (thelist.internet.com) or The Ultimate Web ISP List (webisplist.internetlist.com), both of which list thousands of local and national ISPs. If you need to add a new Windows-based Internet connection (or edit an existing one), use the Internet Connection Wizard (present in Windows 98, or with certain versions of Internet Explorer) or open My Computer, select Dial-Up Networking, and add or edit from there.

Using the PrintMaster Web Site

To get to the PrintMaster Web site, from within PrintMaster, choose the Web menu and select Go To PrintMaster Site. Your Web browser launches, connects you to the Internet, and takes you directly to the site shown in Figure 14.1. (Because PrintMaster is constantly updating its Web site, the pages you see might look slightly different from the pages shown in this book.)

The Direct Address

You can go directly to the PrintMaster Web site at the following Web address: www.printeverything.com/1710_PrintMaster_Reg/ 1710index.html.

Access the PrintEverything site.

Access bonus images.

Shop for other PrintMaster products.

Send an email greeting.

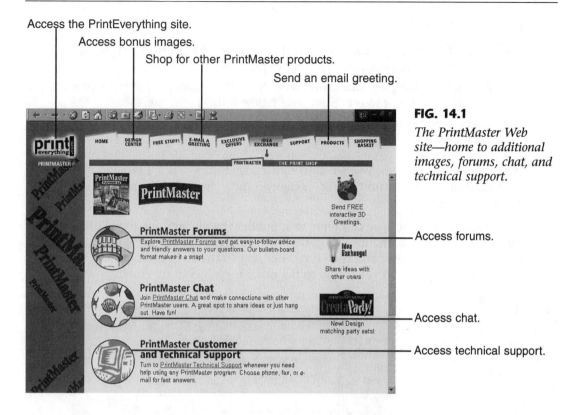

FIG. 14.1

The PrintMaster Web site—home to additional images, forums, chat, and technical support.

Access forums.

Access chat.

Access technical support.

From this main page, you can access links to forums, chat, technical support, additional images, additional graphics products, and email greetings.

The first time you access the PrintMaster site you are prompted to register a new account. Registration is free—just fill in all the blanks (and make up a password), as requested, and then click the Register button. On subsequent visits, you'll go directly to the main page; no additional registration required.

PrintMaster Forums

Forums are like electronic bulletin boards, where you can exchange messages with other PrintMaster users on a variety of PrintMaster-related topics. You access PrintMaster's forums by clicking the PrintMaster Forums link on the PrintMaster home page.

Three main forums are available:

➤ **Hints & Tricks Forum.** Users in this forum exchange their best tips and secrets for jazzing up their PrintMaster projects.

➤ **Project Posting Forum.** This forum lets you display your favorite projects— and view the best projects from your fellow PrintMaster users.

➤ **User Supported Help Forum.** Turn here for answers to your PrintMaster questions.

When you enter a forum, you see a list of message topics. Click a topic to view the individual messages within that topic; click an individual message header to read the entire message.

As you read a message, you can reply to it publicly by clicking the Reply link. As you can see in Figure 14.2, the resulting Submit a Message page requires you to enter your name and email address, and then type your text in the large Message box. Click the Post Message box to add your reply to the other messages in this topic.

FIG. 14.2

Replying to a PrintMaster forum message—click the Post Message button to add your message to the list.

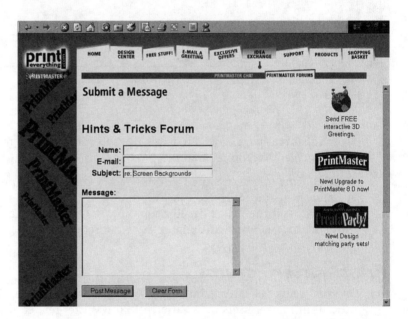

You can create a new message topic by returning to the main forum page and clicking the Submit a Message link. You'll see the same Submit a Message page as you do when replying to a message, but you'll have to enter a new topic in the Subject box.

Post a Project

The Project Posting Forum is a great place to display your PrintMaster projects. You can actually upload your favorite projects for others to see—and view projects uploaded by other PrintMaster users!

To upload a project to the Project Posting Forum, select the Submit a Message link to display the Submit a Message page. The Project Posting Forum has two boxes not found in other forums—the Select File to Upload box and the Enter a Caption for This File box. Click the Browse button to select which file on your hard disk you want to upload (the filename is then automatically placed in the Select File to Upload box) and enter a brief description of the file in the Enter a Caption for This File box. Click the Post Message button to submit your message, with your PrintMaster project file attached.

Visitors to the Project Posting Forum read user messages as normal, although messages in this forum can also include links to uploaded project files. While you're reading a message in this forum, click a project file link to save the file to your hard disk, and then use the PrintMaster program to open and view the downloaded file.

PrintMaster Chat

Chat is real-time communication with other PrintMaster users. When you click the PrintMaster Chat link, you see a series of messages such as the ones shown in Figure 14.3, with the newest at the top. You can enter a message of your own by clicking the Submit a Message link; when the next page appears, enter your Name, E-Mail Address, Subject, and Message. When you click the Post Message button, your message is added to the other messages in the chat list.

FIG. 14.3

Exchanging real-time messages with other PrintMaster users.

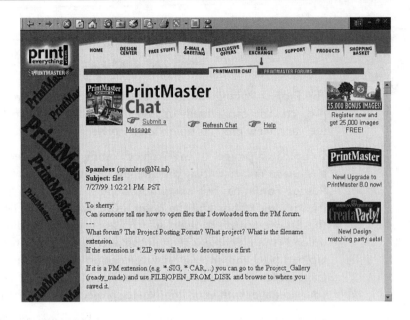

PrintMaster Support

PrintMaster's technical support is integrated into The Learning Company's main support site. This site lists TLC's phone and fax support numbers, and provides links to the following online support options:

- ➤ **On-line Support Request Form.** This option presents a form you can fill out and send (electronically) to the TLC support department, detailing the specific issues you're having with PrintMaster. You should receive an answer to your question within one business day.

- ➤ **FTP Site Support.** This option takes you to TLC's Download site for files you might need to update your version of PrintMaster.

- ➤ **Customer Support FAQ.** This option displays a document that lists answers to frequently asked questions (FAQ), including questions about product returns, rebates, and international orders.

Direct Support

You can access PrintMaster technical support from the PrintMaster Web site, or by going directly to the following address:

`support.learningco.com`.

Additional Images

When you select the Free Stuff tab at the top of the main PrintMaster page, you get access to 25,000 free graphics images. When the Free Stuff page appears, click the 25,000 Free Bonus Images link. You are prompted to register for the bonus images, so follow the onscreen instructions and proceed through the registration process. You'll end up in the TLC Shopping Cart, with the bonus images (at zero cost) listed. Click Check Out to display the Customer and Payment Information page; enter your name, address, and other info, and then click the Submit Order button. When the Thank You for Your Order page appears, click the Continue button to continue to the Art Store.

You Own It, They Store It

When you purchase an art collection from the Art Store (including the bonus collection you get for free), the pictures in the collection reside on the PrintMaster Web site. You can download any image from the collection for free, but you don't actually take possession of a physical collection—unless you choose to download each of the images in the collection individually!

Within the Art Store, you have access to your bonus images, as well as to other images you can download for a fee. To find a specific image, enter a desc____ what you're looking for in the Key Word box, and then cli__ ____ in the main window, as shown in Figure 14-4. ____ ____ free have a check mark next to them. Cl__ ____ ____

Art Store Alter____

You can also access the Art Store by cli__ ____ from anywhere in the PrintMaster site a__ ____ Center icon.

Results of your search—click an image to order and download.

FIG. 14.4

Searching for an image to download from PrintMaster's Art Store.

Enter search phrase here.

Choose to search for images that contain ALL the keywords, or just some (ANY) of the keywords.

Choose which subscriptions to search (purchased, not yet purchased, or both).

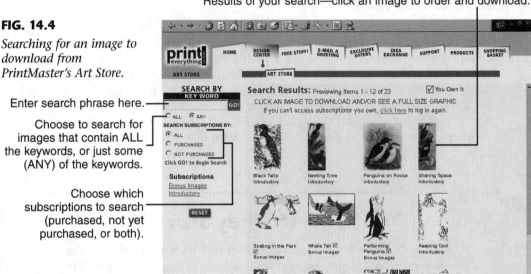

When the Download This Image page appears, you can do one of three things:

➤ Click the Save button to save the image file to your hard disk.

➤ Click the Copy button to copy the image to the Windows Clipboard; you can then return to PrintMaster and use the Paste command to paste the image into your project.

➤ Use your mouse to drag the picture from your Web browser window and drop it into your PrintMaster project.

Download the Plug-In

Before you can view an image on the Download This Image page, you have to download and install the PrintEverything Image Plugin. If you haven't already been prompted to do this, click the Download the PrintEverything Image Plugin link on the Download This Image page, and follow the instructions to download and install the plug-in.

If you select an image that you don't yet own, you are prompted on how to purchase the image collection that contains this specific picture. Follow the onscreen instructions if you want to purchase this collection.

Additional Products

When you click the Products tab on the PrintMaster page, you're taken to the PrintEverything Products page. From here, you can upgrade to the latest version of PrintMaster, or order other products directly from The Learning Company.

Email Greetings

When you click the E-Mail a Greeting tab, you can send electronic greeting cards via email to other Internet users. See Chapter 15, "Send an Online Animated Greeting Card," for more details.

More Resources at PrintEverything

The PrintMaster Web site is actually part of The Learning Company's larger PrintEverything site. When you go directly to www.printeverything.com (or click the PrintEverything logo on the PrintMaster site), you access the main PrintEverything site, which services all graphics products distributed by The Learning Company—including PrintMaster, The Print Shop, American Greetings, and ClickArt.

In the Next Chapter...

Now that you know how to configure PrintMaster for the Internet and access PrintMaster's Web site, it's time to go online—and send some greeting cards! Go to Chapter 15 to learn more.

Send an Online Animated Greeting Card

Online greeting cards are the latest rage. Several sites on the Web let you choose and send these colorful greetings over the Internet—and PrintMaster provides several ways to send online greetings to your friends and family!

Send a 3D Animated Greeting

PrintMaster, in conjunction with 3DGreetings.com, lets you create and send animated multimedia greeting cards—complete with personalized greetings—to anyone on the Internet with an email account. These 3D animated greetings are more than just simple picture postcards—they move and talk and play music, thanks to a special 3D Player that is included with each message you send.

To create an animated email greeting card, click the Browse Animated Greetings button on PrintMaster's File toolbar. This launches your Web browser (without connecting to the Internet) and loads a special Send a 3D Animated Greeting page directly from your hard disk. (With some installations, you might be asked to insert a CD to access this page.)

From the Send a 3D Animated Greeting page, select one of the 10 categories in the left column. This displays all the cards within that category, as shown in Figure 15.1.

FIG. 15.1

A selection of 3D ani-mated greeting cards.

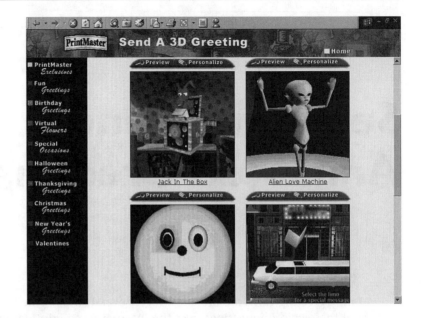

To preview one of the cards—and you have to preview it to get the complete experience—click the Preview button above the card. When the File Download dialog box appears, check the Run This Program from This Current Location option. The 3D greeting file is downloaded and the 3D Player appears on your desktop, as shown in Figure 15.2. Click the Play button to "play" the greeting card.

Internet Explorer Plays, Netscape Navigator Saves

If your Web browser is Internet Explorer, you can preview and play these online greeting cards without actually saving them to your hard disk, as described in the text. However, if you're using Netscape Navigator as your Web browser, you first have to save the greeting card files to your hard disk, and then open them to view them. You'll see a Save As dialog box; select where you want to save the file, and then click the Save button. You can then use either Windows Explorer or My Computer to locate and run the saved file (by clicking or double-clicking it)—which then "plays" the greeting card.

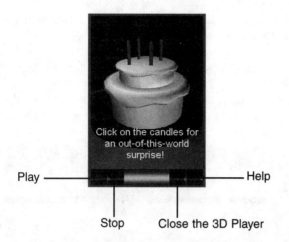

FIG. 15.2

Playing a 3D animated greeting card.

Play — Stop — Close the 3D Player — Help

To personalize and send a card, click the Personalize button above the card. This opens a second Web browser, automatically launches an Internet connection, and takes you to the 3D Animated Greetings Web site. Enter your name, your email address, the recipient's name, the recipient's email address, and your personal message. (You can send a card to multiple recipients by separating the names and addresses with semicolons.) You can also choose whether the card plays with a male or female voice. Click the Send It! button to send the message via email.

Your recipient will receive an email message notifying her that she has a 3DGreeting waiting at 3DGreetings.com; you'll also receive an email informing you that the 3D Greeting has been sent. The message contains a link to the greeting; depending on the recipient's email program, she can either click the link to go directly to the page, or copy the link's URL and paste it into her Web browser.

When she goes to access her greeting, she'll follow the onscreen instructions to prepare the card and download it to her PC. After downloading the card (and the 3D Player), the recipient clicks the Play button to play the greeting. Your personal message is displayed on top of the 3D Player.

Send an Online Postcard from the PrintMaster Web Site

You can also send online greetings from the PrintMaster Web site. When you choose PrintMaster's Web menu and select Go to PrintMaster site (or go directly to www.printeverything.com), click the E-Mail a Greeting tab. This displays the E-Mail a Greeting page, which has two options:

➤ **Send a 3D Greeting.** This takes you to an online version of PrintMaster's Send a 3D Animated Greeting page (with newer cards available). This online version works similarly to the version with PrintMaster; follow the onscreen instructions to choose, personalize, and send animated greetings.

➤ **Send a Postcard.** An online postcard includes colorful graphics and a personalized message—and is sent via normal email.

To create and send an online postcard, click the Send a Postcard link to display the Send a Postcard page, shown in Figure 15.3. From this page, select the postcard you want to send, add your personal message, enter the recipient's name and email address and your name and email address, and then click the Send Card button.

FIG. 15.3

Select, personalize, and send an electronic postcard via email.

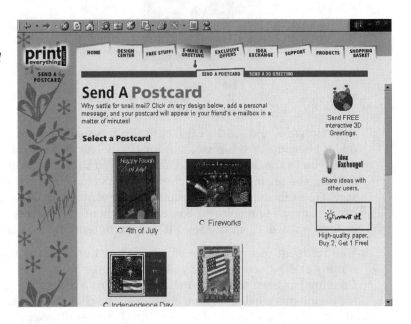

Your recipient will receive an email message notifying him that a postcard is waiting for him at PrintEverything.com. The message contains a link to the greeting; depending on his email program, the recipient can either click the link to go directly to the page, or copy the link's URL and paste it into his Web browser. The link leads the recipient to the full-size greeting card and message, as shown in Figure 15.4.

Send a PrintMaster Greeting Card via Email

There is one more way to use PrintMaster to send email greetings. You can create a normal greeting card within PrintMaster, but then choose to send the card via email!

It's easy to do. Just create a standard half-fold or quarter-fold greeting card, as you would normally. When the card is finished, choose the File menu and select Send Online Greeting.

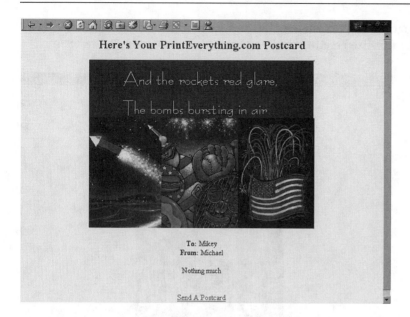

FIG. 15.4

Recipients use their Web browsers to view their PrintEverything postcards.

When the Send Online Greeting dialog box appears (see Figure 15.5), enter your email address in the From box, the recipient's email address in the To box, and a title for your greeting in the Subject box. Use the calendar to select the date you want to send the card, and then click OK.

FIG. 15.5

Tell PrintMaster whom to send your card to—and when.

PrintMaster builds and sends the front and inside pages of your greeting card to its Web site, where it is stored until your recipient "claims" the card. Your recipient receives an email message notifying him that he has a personal greeting card waiting; the message contains a link to the greeting. Your recipient can either click the link to go directly to the page, or copy the link's URL and paste it into his Web browser. The link leads him to the full-size greeting card you created, as shown in Figure 15.6.

FIG. 15.6

A PrintMaster greeting card, viewed online—scroll down and click the Open Card button to read the inside of the card.

If you scheduled a future delivery of a card, you'll receive an email from PrintMaster two days in advance, reminding you of the pending delivery. If you change your mind about sending a card, all you have to do is choose PrintMaster's File menu and select Cancel a Scheduled Online Greeting. This takes you to the Scheduled Card Manager at the PrintMaster Web site. Choose the card or recipient you want to cancel, and PrintMaster cancels the scheduled delivery.

In the Next Chapter...

The Official PrintMaster Guide is almost done, and there's one—just one—type of project remaining. Turn to the final chapter, Chapter 16, "Create and Publish Personal Web Pages," to learn how to use PrintMaster to create and publish your own personal Web pages!

Create and Publish Personal Web Pages

Over 300 million individual pages exist on the World Wide Web—including tens of millions of personal and small business Web pages, created by people just like you. Now, with PrintMaster 8.0, it's easy to create your own simple Web pages—and post them to your own personal site on the Web!

A Very Short Web Page Primer

Web pages are viewed with Web *browsers*. The most popular browser programs are Netscape Navigator and Microsoft Internet Explorer. You probably have one (or both) of these programs already installed on your PC.

Building a Web Page—With HTML

A Web page is nothing more than a computer file composed in a certain language or *code*. Just like any other file you create with PrintMaster, a Web page file consists of various elements (text and graphics) arranged against a background.

In addition to text and graphics, Web pages can also include *hyperlinks* to other Web pages. When users click a hyperlink, they automatically jump to the linked page. Hyperlinks can connect Web pages on the same site or on different sites—even in different countries!

The code used to create a Web page document is called *HTML*, which stands for Hypertext Markup Language. The codes in HTML work in the background to define what you see when you view a Web page from your Netscape Navigator or Internet Explorer Web browser.

When you create a Web page with PrintMaster, you never see the underlying HTML code. PrintMaster does all the work for you, converting your document into the proper HTML code, and keeping the code completely in the background. All you see is the Web project you're working on; all Web servers see is your finished Web page.

More About HTML Code

PrintMaster keeps the HTML code for your Web pages in the background; you never even see the code, let alone get the opportunity to edit it manually. However, there are some sophisticated Web page effects that can be added only by directly editing the HTML code. Because PrintMaster doesn't let you edit the code, you can't add these effects from within PrintMaster.

If you want to edit the HTML code in your PrintMaster Web pages, you first need to publish your pages to a folder (*not* to the Web—at least, not yet!). You do this by choosing the Web menu, selecting Publish to Folder, and then following the onscreen instructions to save the page to your hard disk in HTML format.

After the file has been saved, you can use separate *HTML editor* software to open and edit the HTML code. You can find some of the best HTML editors at the ZDNet Software library, at `www.zdnet.com/swlib/hotfiles/10html.html`; your local computer store should also have a wide selection of HTML editors for sale. You might even have an HTML editor already installed on your system—the Netscape Composer editor is included as part of the Netscape Communicator suite, and the FrontPage Express editor is included with both Microsoft Windows 98 and Internet Explorer.

After you've finished editing the raw HTML code, you can then post your pages to your hosting service, as described later in this chapter.

If you want to learn more about HTML editing, check out The HTML Tutor (`html.cavalcade-whimsey.com`) or HTML Goodies (`www.htmlgoodies.com`) on the Web. You can also pick up a copy of *The Complete Idiot's Guide to Creating an HTML 4 Web Page* wherever good books are sold, which is a great primer for creating your own Web pages with HTML.

Web Page Addresses

A Web address—otherwise known as a *URL*, or *Uniform Resource Locator*—precisely points to a single Web page. The first part of the URL is the **http://**, which tells Web browsers that what follows is a Web page. (There are other prefixes for other types of Internet sites—**ftp://** for FTP sites, for example—but these are used less frequently.) Following the prefix, in most instances, is the site address, in the form of **www.***site***.com**. This form is *not* a standard; site addresses can start with something other than **www.** and end with something other than **.com**. (For example, sites for nonprofit organizations often end in **.org**, government sites end in **.gov**, and sites from other countries end in specific country codes.)

When you enter a site address, you are automatically taken to the home page of that site. In most cases, the home page has an address that looks like this: **www.***site***.com/index.html**. You don't have to enter the **index.html**, because Web browsers automatically look for and load the **index.html** page when you just enter a site address.

If a site has a lot of pages, the pages might be organized into *directories*, with each directory representing a specific topic or branch. Each directory is preceded by the "backslash" symbol, and the directory's contents (including any subdirectories within the directory) follow a backslash.

So, if you had the directory **frank** on our hypothetical site, its address would be **www.***site***.com/frank/**. If the **frank** directory had another subdirectory named **bob** that contained the **bob.html** page, the address for that page would be **www.***site***.com/frank/bob/bob.html**.

Posting and Hosting

For a Web page to be viewed by other users, however, that page must reside on a *Web server*, a computer continuously connected to the Internet. When a Web page is *hosted* by a server, that page receives its own specific address; you have to *post* or *publish* your page to the host server.

When you have more than one page together on a server, you have a *Web site*. Again, anybody can create a Web site; the pros just build bigger and fancier sites than do normal folks like you or me.

To summarize, here are the steps you need to take to create your own personal page on the Web:

1. Use PrintMaster to create your page(s).
2. Find a Web site to host your page(s).
3. Publish your page(s) to your Web-hosting service.

Now let's get to it—and start creating your very first Web page!

Starting a New Web Page

There are three ways to start a new Web page: via a ready-made project, using the With Help Designer, and completely from scratch.

Creating a Ready-Made Web Page

To select from one of PrintMaster's 44 ready-made Web pages, follow these steps:

1. From the Hub, select Ready-Made.

2. When the Project Gallery appears, choose the Project Type list and select Web Pages.

3. Select a page from either the Business, Community, or Personal categories, and then click the Select button. See Figure 16.1 for an example of PrintMaster's ready-made Web pages.

FIG. 16.1

A ready-made Web page, ready for editing—don't forget to insert the hyper-links!

Creating a Web Page Using With Help

To use the With Help Designer to create a Web page, follow these steps:

1. From the Hub, select With Help.

2. When the With Help Designer appears, select Web Page and click Next.

3. When the next page of the Designer appears, select what type of page you want (Business, Community, or Personal); then click Next.

4. When the next page of the Designer appears, select what style of page you want (Classic, Contemporary, or Whimsical), and then click Next.

5. When the final page of the Designer appears, click Finish.

You're now presented with a Web page template (as shown in Figure 16.2), complete with dummy text and graphics, ready for editing.

FIG. 16.2
A Web page template created with the With Help Designer.

How Wide?

How wide should you make your Web page? If you want to be absolutely sure that every user on the Web can see all your page without scrolling left or right, select PrintMaster's Standard width; this sizes your page to fit on standard VGA monitors with 640×480 pixel resolution. Because most users today are running their systems at higher resolutions (putting more of the picture on the screen), you might want to select PrintMaster's Wide option; this sizes your page to fit on monitors running 800×600 pixel resolution. It is probably unwise to opt for a greater width, because fewer users will be able to see the entire width of your page without scrolling.

Creating a Brand-New Web Page

To create a blank Web page from scratch, follow these steps:

1. From the Hub, select Brand New.

2. When the New Project dialog box appears, select Web Page, and then click Next.

3. When the Web Page Setup dialog box appears, select the Page Width (Standard, Wide, or Custom), select the page Height (and Width, if you selected the preceding Custom option), and then click Finish.

You now see a blank Web page, ready for editing.

199

Editing Your Web Page

Each page of your Web site can include graphics, photos, and text, plus links to other Web pages and even other Web sites. You can edit the size of your page, the page's background color, and all the elements you place on the page. In fact, editing a Web page is just like editing any other PrintMaster project; PrintMaster automatically converts whatever you design into the proper HTML code to place on the Web.

Add a Background

PrintMaster lets youselect either a background color, texture (pattern), or graphic for the background of your Web page. Just choose the Web menu and select Page Properties to display the Web Page Properties dialog box (see Figure 16.3).

FIG. 16.3

Change your page's background in the Web Page Properties dialog box.

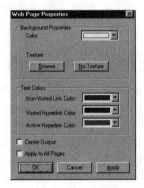

To use a solid color background, select a color from the Color list. To use a patterned or graphic background, click the Browse button; this displays the Web Art Gallery. Select Backgrounds from the Category list, select a background graphic, and then click Select to return to the Page Properties dialog box. (Note that all background graphics are "tiled" down the length of a Web page.)

If you want your background to be the same across all pages in your site, check the Apply to All Pages option. If you want to remove a background graphic, click the No Texture button. Click OK when finished.

Graphic, No Color

If you select a background graphic, that automatically overrides (and covers up) the background color.

Add Text

Adding text to a Web page is just like adding text to any other PrintMaster project; you insert a text box and then enter and format your text.

There are, however, some differences in how your text is displayed on the Web. First, not all text formatting converts to the HTML code used to create a Web page. Any text that has been stretched, rotated, shadowed, or filled in with a pattern won't convert to HTML. If you apply these formats, your text will actually be converted to a graphic on your Web page, which means it appears as a *picture* of text, rather than editable text itself.

Is Text-As-Graphic Bad?

Avoid converting too much of your text to graphics, because graphics take up more file space and take longer to download. On the other hand, displaying text as a graphic ensures that all visitors to your page will see your text exactly as designed. You'll need to weigh the trade-off of slower downloading versus more accurate representation when you're considering whether to allow your text to be converted to a graphic.

Although PrintMaster automatically converts overly formatted text into a graphic for Web publishing, you do have some control over how your text is converted. Begin by right-clicking a text box, and then selecting HTML Format from the pop-up menu. From here, you can make the following selections:

➤ **Automatic.** This enables PrintMaster to convert the text to a graphic if necessary.

➤ **Keep As Text.** This tells PrintMaster to not convert the text to a graphic; some formatting might be lost when your page is published.

➤ **Publish As Graphic.** This automatically converts the text to a graphic, no matter what formatting is applied.

You also want to avoid using tabs in your text. HTML converts tabs into spaces, with varying results.

Add Graphics

Although you can use standard PrintMaster graphics in your Web pages, PrintMaster includes a special Web Art Gallery with graphics specially configured to look good and download fast on a Web page. You access the Web Art Gallery (shown in Figure 16.4) by choosing the Add menu and selecting Web Art.

FIG. 16.4

Select artwork optimized for the Web from the Web Art Gallery.

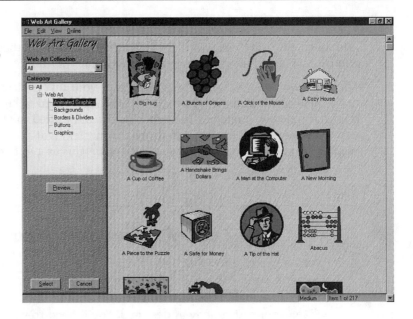

The Web Art Gallery includes

➤ Animated Graphics

➤ Backgrounds

➤ Borders & Dividers

➤ Buttons

➤ Graphics

When you're adding art to your Web page, keep in mind that on the Web, overlapping elements are turned into a single graphic element. This won't affect how the graphics look, but can increase the download time of your Web page.

Animated Graphics

On the Web, you can use *animated graphics*—a single graphic file that alternates between multiple images, like a crude animation. PrintMaster's Web Art Gallery includes an entire Animated Graphics category; to see how an animated graphic will look on your Web page, click a thumbnail, and then click Preview. Click Done to end the preview.

Add a Hyperlink

You can make any piece of text or graphic a hyperlink to another Web page. When users click the hyperlink, they jump to the page you specify when you're designing your Web page.

To add a hyperlink to text on your page, begin by highlighting that text. (You have to highlight the individual words and letters, *not* the entire text box.) Now choose the Web menu and select Hyperlink.

When the Hyperlink dialog box appears (as shown in Figure 16.5), check the type of link you want to create from the following:

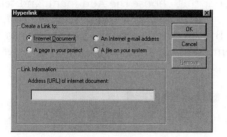

FIG. 16.5

Add a hyperlink to your project via the Hyperlink dialog box.

➤ **Internet Document.** This lets you link to another page on the Web. When you select this option (which is the most common type of hyperlink), enter the full URL of the other page—including the **http://**—in the Link Information box.

➤ **A Page in Your Project.** This lets you link to another Web page you've created with PrintMaster. When you select this option, indicate which page of your project you want to link to.

➤ **An Internet E-Mail Address.** This lets you create a link to your email address; when a user clicks on this type of link, his or her email program automatically launches and addresses a message to your email account. When you select this option, enter your full email address in the Link Information box.

➤ **A File on Your System.** This little-used type of hyperlink lets you link to a file on your PC; users must have the same program installed on their PC to view the file. When you select this option, enter the full path of the file on your hard disk in the Link Information box.

When you click OK, the text you selected now appears underlined, indicating an active hyperlink. To remove a hyperlink, just delete the underlined words.

You can also create a hyperlink to any nontext area on your Web page. This type of graphical hyperlink is called a *hot spot*. It's common to create hot spots on top of buttons that you want users to "click," or parts of graphics that you want to link to other pages.

To create a hot spot, choose the Web menu and select Create Hot Spot; your cursor now changes shape. Move the cursor to the beginning of the area you want to link, and draw a box around the area. (The hot spot box looks and behaves just like any other PrintMaster element, complete with handles you can use to resize, reposition, and rotate the hot spot.) When you release the mouse button, the Hyperlink dialog box appears. Fill in the hyperlink information as previously discussed, and then click OK.

Add a New Page

If you have a lot of information to present, you probably want to do it on multiple Web pages. (Making a page too long requires users to do a lot of scrolling, which is a bother.) To add another page to your site, choose the Add menu and select Pages; when the Add Pages dialog box appears, select how many pages to add, whether you want to add them before or after the current page, and whether you want to add a blank page or a copy of the current page. Click OK to add the new page(s).

Ten Tips for Better Web Pages

Here are some of my favorite tips for making better-looking and faster-loading Web pages.

Tip #1: Minimize Scrolling

Web surfers don't like to scroll through long pages. If your page is getting too long (requiring more than two full scrolls, as a rule of thumb), break it up by adding a second page and putting some of your information there.

Tip #2: Use Text Instead of Graphics

Some of the most popular sites on the Web are mainly text, and use few graphics. (Look at Yahoo!—www.yahoo.com—as an example.) This is because text loads faster than graphics, and Web surfers hate to wait for a page to load. If you can say it in text, do so—and keep the graphics to a minimum.

Tip #3: Minimize the Size of Your Graphics

In general, smaller graphics are better on the Web. Smaller graphics load faster, and users don't like to spend a lot of time waiting for all the elements of a page to load. It's worth the effort to resize and crop larger graphics to take up the minimum amount of space possible on your page.

Tip #4: Use Thumbnails to Represent Larger Graphics

If you absolutely must include large graphics on your site, you don't have to put them full-size on your main page. Instead, insert smaller versions of your pictures (called *thumbnails*) on your page, and draw hotspots around them and link to the larger pictures that have been published separately. This way, casual surfers aren't burdened by long download times on your main page, and more interested surfers can click to see the full-size versions.

Tip #5: Use a Consistent Design for Multiple Pages

If you have multiple pages on your site, use the same overall design for all the pages. That means using the same background, the same page layout, and the same text font. Users like a consistency in look and feel (and navigation).

Tip #6: Lighter Backgrounds Are Better

Lighter backgrounds, as well as simpler backgrounds, are better. In fact, a plain white page is perfectly okay on the Web. It's tough trying to read light text on a dark background; dark text against a light background is easier on the eyes.

As to background simplicity, avoid using background textures or graphics that clutter up your pages. Again, it's difficult to read text against a cluttered background. Keep it simple!

Tip #7: Use Common Fonts

Just because you have a fancy font installed on your PC doesn't mean the people visiting your Web page have the same font installed on their PCs. (And if they don't, your page might not display properly.) You need to hit a "lowest common denominator" in terms of fonts used, so all visitors can view your page properly. Stick to common fonts such as Arial, Courier, and Times New Roman. And be conservative on your type *sizes*, too—stick to text between 10 and 30 points.

Tip #8: Don't Change Link Colors—Or Use Underlined Text

Because hyperlinks automatically appear underlined on your page, users think that any underlined text is a hyperlink. If you underline *nonhyperlinked* text, you'll do nothing but confuse your site visitors. (Can you imagine them clicking, clicking, clicking some underlined text trying to make it link somewhere?) If you need to emphasize a word, use boldface or italic—and avoid underlining!

Tip #9: Include Your Email Address

Visitors to your site might want to contact you—to ask you questions, or compliment you on your site. For this reason, it's a good idea to include a link to your email address at the bottom of your page.

Tip #10: Keep It Simple!

On the Web, simpler is better. Use simple backgrounds, simple page layouts, and simple text and graphics. Leave a lot of "whitespace" for readability. And be sure that the navigation from page to page is simple and intuitive. Don't try to impress visitors with your design brilliance—keep it simple and create a usable site!

Publishing Your Web Page to the Internet

After you've created your Web page, you need to save it and *publish* it to the Internet so that other Web users can view it. To publish your page, you first have to find a Web-hosting service and establish a membership there. The host site should provide you with the *uploading* information you need to publish your pages properly.

Find a Host

There are several places to look for a Web site to host your Web pages. First, your Internet service provider might provide Web-hosting services—and typically at low or no cost. Second, the company you work for—or the school you attend—might permit employee/student Web pages to be hosted on its servers. Third, you can check out one of the personal page communities on the Web; these communities host pages from millions of users. Some of the more popular personal page communities are

➤ Angelfire (www.angelfire.com)

➤ AOL Hometown (hometown.aol.com)—for America Online subscribers only

➤ GeoCities (www.geocities.com)

➤ The Globe (www.theglobe.com)

➤ Tripod (www.tripod)

Most of these personal home page sites don't charge any fees to host your personal pages. They make their money from selling advertising; you get one or more free Web pages as part of the bargain.

Finally, there are numerous *commercial* hosting services, designed to host larger and business-oriented Web sites. These services typically charge a fee, but offer more storage space and hosting options. See the FINDaHOST (www.findahost.com) or HostSearch (www.hostsearch.com) sites for lists of these services.

Before You Publish—Check and Preview Your Design

Before you publish your page, you should check to see how it actually works in HTML—how elements convert, and how long it takes to load the page. You do this by running PrintMaster's Design Checker.

You run the Design Checker by choosing the Web menu and selecting Design Checker. The Design Checker now saves your project in HTML and performs a series of checks against the HTML code. When it is finished checking your project, it displays a Web Page Design Checker dialog box (such as the one shown in Figure 16.6) that tells you how long each page takes to load, and presents any issues it found in converting your project to HTML. Follow the advice in the dialog box to edit your project and create faster-loading pages.

FIG. 16.6

Use the Design Checker to help you optimize your Web pages.

After you've used the Design Checker, you should take a look at your pages as they'll actually look on the Web. Fortunately, PrintMaster lets you display a preview of your pages in your own Web browser (either Internet Explorer or Netscape Navigator)—*before* you publish the pages on the Web itself!

To preview your project, choose the Web menu and select Preview Web Site. PrintMaster now converts your project to HTML format, launches your Web browser, and displays your Web pages (as shown in Figure 16.7).

While you're previewing your pages, check out the appearance of all your design elements (including text), and test all the hyperlinks and hotspots. When you're finished with the preview, close your Web browser.

FIG. 16.7

Preview your pages in a Web browser—this is how they'll look on the Internet.

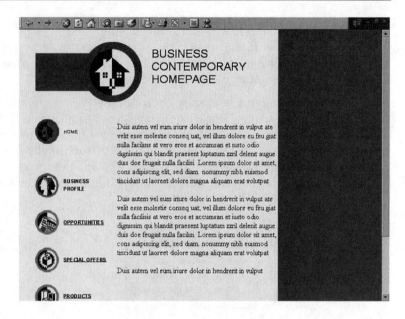

Publish to Your Hard Disk

You might want to temporarily store your Web pages on your hard disk without posting them to the Internet. To save your pages—in HTML format—on your own system, choose the Web menu and select Publish to Folder. When the Choose Directory dialog box appears, select the directory where you want to store your page(s), and then click OK.

Getting Published

After you're satisfied with the way your Web page looks and performs, you're ready to post the page to the Web. Choose the Web menu and select Publish to Web Site. When the PrintMaster Confirmation box appears, click Yes.

PrintMaster now converts your project to HTML format, and then runs the Design Checker one more time. When the Web Page Design Checker dialog box appears, click Continue.

208

Change the Name

In most instances, the name of your main Web page is **index.html.** If your Web hosting service assigns a different name to your page, choose the Web menu and select Web Publishing Properties; when the Web Publishing Properties dialog box appears, enter a new name or file extension, as appropriate, and then click OK.

Now PrintMaster launches the Microsoft Web Publishing Wizard. This wizard leads you step-by-step through the tasks necessary to publish your page(s) on the Web. The wizard needs to know the name of the host Web server, as well as the URL assigned to your main page. If you don't have all this information, get it from your Web-hosting service. (You might also be asked for your username and password, both of which should be assigned by your Web-hosting service.) Follow the onscreen instructions to finish publishing your page.

When the Web Publishing Wizard is done, your page(s) are posted on the Web, displayed for the entire Internet to see!

Master of Your Domain

When you post your page to a hosting service, it is automatically assigned a URL by the service—you have little or no control over the address you get assigned, and it's typically a long address several directories down from the host's primary domain name. It's possible, however, to obtain your own personal domain name—so that your Web page address reads www.*mydomain*.com. To obtain a personal domain name, check first with your Web-page hosting service; most services and ISPs can do all the legwork for you. You can also use a separate registration service, such as Register.com (www.register.com), or you can register directly with the official Network Solutions site (www.networksolutions.com). Note, however, that obtaining a personal domain name takes a bit of time (you have some forms to fill in) and costs a bit of money (typically $35 or so per year).

Other Ways to Create Web Pages with PrintMaster

In addition to the standard Web pages just described, PrintMaster has two more ways to create HTML pages on the Web—by converting other PrintMaster projects to HTML, and through Photo Organizer's Picture Web Page function.

Convert Almost Any PrintMaster Project to HTML

PrintMaster lets you publish most types of PrintMaster projects—cards, certificates, invitations, even crafts—to the Internet. When you choose to publish a project, PrintMaster automatically converts the project to the HTML code necessary to create a Web page.

From within any PrintMaster project, choose the Web menu and select Publish to Web Site. When the PrintMaster Confirmation box appears, click Yes. PrintMaster now converts your project to HTML format, and then runs the Design Checker. When the Web Page Design Checker dialog box appears, click Continue. When PrintMaster launches the Microsoft Web Publishing Wizard, continue as instructed in the Getting Published section of this chapter.

Create a Picture Web Page with Photo Organizer

PrintMaster's Photo Organizer tool includes an option to create Photo Web Pages. These pages are essentially photo albums on the Web, with thumbnails linking to full-sized pictures. To learn how to create Photo Web Pages, turn to Chapter 8, "Better Pictures and Photographs."

What Comes Next...

This concludes the final chapter in *The Official PrintMaster Guide*. Throughout this book, you've learned how to use PrintMaster to create a variety of projects, and how to make those projects look terrific. Now it's time to close the book, and start using PrintMaster—like a pro!

Index

D

HERE'S WHAT THE CRITICS ARE SAYING...

Family PC

- "Our testers are notoriously hard to please, but...they give this comprehensive product a 91 score, making it the highest-rated publishing program in the five-year history of Family Testing."
- "...complete and exhaustive program"
- "PrintMaster Platinum is bursting at the seams with features..."
- "...it's easy to navigate and use"

National Parenting Center

- "This everything-in-a-box software will astound you as it did our testers. It contains a vast array of ideas, templates and fun."
- "The results are absolutely top notch and the easy-to-use, intuitive navigation is a snap!"

Universal Press Syndicate

- "PrintMaster Platinum 8.0 from Broderbund looks so good it has become my favorite for making greeting cards and invitations."